Moving On!
LIVING LIFE TO THE FULLEST AFTER DIVORCE

LaShon F. Williams

PURE PRAISE PUBLISHING
P.O. BOX 4012
SOUTHFIELD, MICHIGAN 48037

Moving On!
Living Life to the Fullest After Divorce
Copyright© 2007 LaShon F. Williams

Unless otherwise stated, all Scripture quotations are from
The Layman's Parallel Bible Version of the Bible.
Copyright © 1991, by Zondervan Publishing House
All emphasis within italics are the author's addition.

ISBN 0-9740877-2-6

Printed in the United States of America. All rights reserved under International Copyright law. No part of this book may be reproduced or transmitted in any form or by any means; electronic, mechanical, including photocopying and recording, or by any information storage and retrieval system, without permission in writing from the publisher.

Cover Designand & Layout: Larry T. Jordan, Pure Praise Media
Editing and Proofing: Bellyfire Media, Detroit, MI.

Published by:
Pure Praise Publishing
P.O. Box 4012
Southfield, Michigan 48037

Printed in the United States of America

Table Of Contents

Table Of Contents	III
Dedication	1
Acknowledgements	3
Preface	5
The Auditions	11
Let's Dance	17
Oh Boy! A Wedding!	29
Everything In Between	39
True Confessions	45
The Beginning of the End	57
The Other Person	69
Revelation(s)	87
"What God Has Joined…"	93
Stages of Recovery	99
Making the Move	127
Steps to Recovery	133
About Us	139

Dedication

To my son, who through no fault of his own has had to endure his parents' divorce.

To all the children of the world who have had to endure their parents' divorces.

Acknowledgements

"Do not grow weary in doing good, for at the proper time you will reap a harvest if you do not give up." Galatians 6:9

 To God be the glory for keeping me when all else failed. For allowing me to go through a divorce and choosing me to share my testimony of recovery. His goodness endureth forever!

 Jay, my little boy, you are growing into my young man. I love you and couldn't be more proud of who you are.

 My parents; Vera Williams and the late Frederick D. Williams for sparing me the pain of divorce as a child. For giving me and my siblings the best childhood ever - through your love, discipline, indescribable sacrifice and family values. I would not be who I am if it weren't for what you've done for me. Thank you for being my parents.

 My siblings; Eric, Yvette and Tresa. For believing in me and encouraging me to write this book. That I needed to do this because my story was worth telling.

 My friend, Traniece, for being there for me through all the difficult times, the late night calls and always speaking the word of the Lord when I wanted to give up.

 Donna, my surrogate mother, I appreciate our friendship and

I thank God for bringing you into my life, our relationship is more than unique - it's special.

Aunt Minnie thanks for sharing your story and words of encouragement and support. I know you know what I mean.

Mary, for always speaking the truth, no matter what. For believing in me and in Divorce Recovery Today, Inc.

Tamela, you have been an incredible help and support from the beginning of Divorce Recovery Today, Inc. I am forever grateful for all your IT knowledge.

Eddie Allen, my editor. We met through Moving On! But it seems like we've known each other longer. Thanks for your professionalism and creativity.

My cousins; Holli and Bridget, for the listening ear and words of encouragement.

Pastor Larry Jordan, for seeing the passion I had for divorce recovery and believing in me. Even when you had your doubts, you supported me beyond measure. Thank you for all you've done for Divorce Recovery Today, Inc.

Janice, co-worker, writer and friend. Thanks for all the editing advice.

Gail Perry-Mason, for your professional advice and support.

To all my *Make a Fresh Start...On the Road to Recovery*" workshop participants. You took the step of faith!

Preface

It took me seven years to decide to write this book, and another two years to put words on paper. Why? I didn't think anyone would believe my story. Stuff like this doesn't happen everyday, or so I thought. It takes courage to write the details of your most intimate moments of heartache and pain, and to make those details available for everyone to read and judge. People get married and divorced everyday and move on. But some don't.

Some can't.

Some won't.

What makes my story so different? Read on and see for yourself.

* * *

I was blown away when my pastor husband, after three-plus years of marriage announced, "We have to get a divorce."

What? Why? What did he mean, "We have to get a divorce?" This could not be happening to me. This would not happen to me.

I never saw it coming: She was a member of the choir. We were casual acquaintances and members of the same sorority, but I barely noticed her. This plain, homely looking woman stole the heart and mind of my husband. He noticed her and before I noticed a thing, my husband, the assistant pastor of our church and the father of my child, had left our home and moved into hers.

He never missed a beat...at least not in the pulpit. Every Sunday morning he was there as the dutiful, caring minister being groomed for a church of his own. The congregation took him in with open arms and defended his every move. Literally They even defended him with a physical move – to a new position as senior pastor of his own church.

Our story played out like a scene from a well-put-together script written for the self- righteous "churched folk" of our small urban city. This is the story of how I survived and overcame the devastation divorce had on my life and the stigma that was attached to it in the church. I thought church folk didn't get divorced. Sure they do. Perhaps the rules just appear to be a little different when you're the pastor.

What does God have to say about divorce? Has the church's response to divorce changed as the divorce rate among Christians rises? Statistics show that 45 to 50 percent of first-time marriages end in divorce. That is equivalent to about half. Another study shows one out of three marriages end in divorce during the first 10 years of the marriage. What is even more alarming is the percentage of re-marriages that end in divorce. Even though 95 percent of divorced individuals re-marry, 76 percent of all second marriages fail, and the number continues to climb from there, according to the internationally known DivorceCare support group. Is divorce still viewed as taboo or an unforgivable sin among churchgoers? Are you doomed to hell because of it?

Looking back at that time in my life, I saw more and more marriages ending in divorce. People masking the pain on the outside, yet broken beyond repair on the inside. When we go through something as painful and personal as a divorce, or any emotional loss for that matter, a transformation takes place. Our reaction is often to turn inward, keep it private and not let anyone know how we really feel. They might use it against us, judge us, pity us, or shun our presence. We try our best to carry on with business as usual, smiling, laughing and putting on the biggest imaginable facade. But in private, we're having this tremendous battle between the emotional reactions and the reality of what is going on around us.

People masking the pain on the outside, yet broken beyond repair on the inside.

If you're reading this book to better understand a relative, friend or co-worker who has gone through a divorce, first, let me commend you for loving and caring about that person enough to take the time. Now let me give you an example of what that person's world may feel like. Have you ever been in an empty tunnel? Try standing in the middle of one and say something out loud. Then listen to the resounding echo. That emptiness is eerie. Creepy, even. The world becomes this empty tunnel for thousands who experience divorce like I did. I was in the tunnel all by myself. For two years I stayed locked there. Many remain locked in a tunnel of mental anguish and emotional devastation long after their marriages end, simply because they can't find a way out.

Divorce is an epidemic that is growing at an unprecedented rate among all nationalities and religions.

This mental tunnel has become a home for men, women and children who experience the emptiness and isolation that divorce can bring. It wasn't until I mentally walked out of my "tunnel" that I realized I must write this book. Divorce is an epidemic that is growing at an unprecedented rate among all nationalities and religions. What does this say about our ability to live together as husbands and wives? What kind of ripple effect is it having on our children and the generation following theirs? What value do we place on marriage and family?

We have support groups for every addiction or issue you can think of. Corporations and businesses have employee groups or facilities available to address everything from childcare to mental illness. For something to have become so commonplace as divorce has in our society, you would think there would be more helpful information on bookshelves. Divorce has become a national epidemic, and I don't think we have acknowledged the fact that it's having an immeasurable effect on our population and culture. By picking up this book, you have acknowledged its personal impact on you or someone you care about, and hopefully you plan to do something about it.

This is not just another self-help guide; it is my personal story – told in a way that can help you consider the concerns, obstacles and approaches you'll need to examine in getting through what's probably one of the most difficult periods in your life. All of the events I'm sharing with you are true; only some names have been changed out of respect for rights and privacy. Let me warn you: This book comes with some requirements. First and foremost, it requires you to be honest with yourself. Nothing and

This process is like a cleansing mechanism.

no one is going to help you if you aren't honestly ready to receive the help you need to recover. In being honest, there are going to be things you discover that you may not like or want to identify yourself with. Don't let that stop you, because it has stopped you for too long already. I want you to use *Moving On!* as your personal map to freedom. Moving from destination to destination is, after all, the purpose of using maps anyway. This map to freedom will help you clear out the disdain in your life, the past hurts and failures, the negative thoughts and bitterness. It will give you the ability to explore something new – anything new.

Moving On! will identify the common stages of divorce recovery. As with recovery from alcohol or drugs, there is a healing process every divorcee should undergo. This process is like a cleansing mechanism. The eventual cleansing is why it's so important to allow yourself to experience denial, admit loneliness, embrace acceptance and eventually walk in forgiveness. These things are required in order for you to Move On! and make a fresh start. Through my experiences and challenges I will share recommendations on how to start over and build positive, productive relationships by eliminating unhealthy influences from your inner circle. Use my story as a reference, returning to it as often as necessary to keep from looking behind you; instead looking forward with hope and vision for your life. This book can be your blueprint to a place of contentment that you never would have thought you could reach. In order to get there, you will have to answer key questions about yourself, your relationships and how you view others. As with reaching other goals, we don't always get it right the first time. So, if no one has ever told you, it's OK to try again. In fact, trying until you get it right is your only choice in finding true healing.

Moving On! Living Life to the Fullest after Divorce will help you to see yourself the way the Creator does. He does not see you through the lens of a broken past, unhappy childhood or repeated mistakes. He does not see ruined or damaged goods. He sees the wonderful person of purpose He conceived long before you were born and before your misfortunes in life occurred. He wants you to see the same.

ONE

THE AUDITIONS

THINK ABOUT IT: *We often make our biggest mistakes during the times when we are least fulfilled. Even the most intelligent people among us may let their guards down when things get dull, or when they are discouraged about certain areas of their lives. Ever notice? We run up credit card debt at the shopping mall because we find ourselves with extra time on our hands. We overeat and pack on pounds, instead of addressing the stress that makes us seek "comfort food." Or maybe we spend less time with our children after we meet the first adult whose kept us company in a long time. As you begin your journey to recovery from separation and divorce, be careful not to make rash and costly choices just to avoid the challenge of transitioning into a new lifestyle. Choices we make out of simple boredom, loneliness or desperation are the ones that most often come back to haunt us.*

I didn't want to stay at that job a minute past five. As I turned the key in my car's ignition, filing in line behind the vehicles headed toward the highway, I dwelled on the single most agonizing thought I'd had every day since my six-month review: "I hate this job! What am I doing here?"

The sound of my supervisor's voice resonated in my ear:

"Now LaShon, you're still on probation and if you don't show some grave improvement within the next six weeks, we are going to be forced to let you go." She kept looking down at her pudgy arms and the stubby fingers crossed in front of her chest. Six months earlier she'd undergone gastric bypass surgery and it had been successful. She was at least 75 pounds lighter, but I wasn't going to pay her any compliments. I hadn't been properly trained, due to her abrupt absence to undergo the surgery when I was hired.

"What?" I remember thinking. "Just who, exactly, does she think she is talking to?"

I gave her a blank stare as if to tell her, "I know what I am doing." But the truth of the matter was, my first job out of college would soon become history. Challenges at work would eventually be the least of my life's concerns.

Traffic was heavy for a Thursday evening. It was just as well. I needed to unwind and refocus from my mentally stressful day. As I crept along for a few miles in bumper-to-bumper traffic, my mind kept focusing on that job, despite how hard I tried to think of other things. My mother's warning voice echoed in my mind the same way a voice traveling in an empty room does.

"LaShon, I don't think this is the type of work you want to get into," she cautioned. "What happened to broadcast journalism, your major?"

Somewhere between my third and fourth year in college, I'd lost confidence in my dream of becoming a well-known actress or, at minimum, a local news anchor. So I settled for the first money maker that came my way, a position in state social service.

"I need a job now, plus I'm not talking about working there until I retire," I arrogantly replied to Mom.

She did her best to steer me away from social work, since she had spent several difficult years in the field herself. But my last few years of college and post-graduation had taken an abrupt turn. As a financially recovering college student, any full-time position equaled the opportunity for something I desperately needed: money! So when the offer came, I accepted.

As I approached the exit ramp, I tried to clear my mind by fantasizing about the evening's events. Auditions were finally an opportunity to do something outside the normal mundane routine of working exclusively, devoid of any social life. I was traveling on a road of serious disappointments, so I couldn't keep from wondering if these auditions would just be another let-down added to the long list.

The car behind me blew its horn, anxiously urging me to complete my left turn. As I turned into the subdivision, I was greeted by scenery that included the few leaves of orange and red left on the trees. They blew lifelessly in front of the beautifully manicured lawns that lined the residential street leading to Lake in the Woods apartments. I had moved into the secluded complex on the lake a few months earlier after the sudden change that had just occurred in my journey from school into the professional world. My apartment was lined with almond-white carpet, a spacious living room and too much dining room for a single woman who didn't entertain. My sizable bedroom and balcony, with entrances from both the living room and bedroom, added length to the apartment's average size. After five years of living with two, three, sometimes four college roommates, and sharing a bedroom with two sisters before college, I enjoyed this luxury of space that I called home.

As I turned the key in the door I heard my phone ringing. Dropping my packages on the floor, I picked up the phone just as the answering machine clicked on.

"Hi LaShon, it's Sue. Lou says auditions for the play 'Black Voices' start at 7:30."

"Tell him I said thanks," I told my friend, "but I'm not sure if I really want to do this."

"Go check it out. What do you have to lose? If you don't like it, leave," was her response. "Let me know at work tomorrow how it turns out," she said, hanging up.

Uggggh! Why did she mention work?

While walking into my bedroom, I caught my reflection in the hallway mirror. "Yeah," I thought. "What do I have to lose?"

This would be unlike anything I'd ever done. Well, maybe not totally. Given my love for acting and modeling, I was drawn to anything that put me in front of an audience. My passion, however, far outweighed my talents and experience. I'd never participated in any stage performance (unless you count the fifth grade when I had a small part in the school play, and no lines to recite – I just mimed and directed some people across the stage!). But I felt as though I would be fulfilling a desire I'd buried years ago.

You see, back when I was 16, I convinced Mom to take me to a local modeling agency. The ad read, "Looking for young girls who want to get started in a modeling career." I was tall, thin and, from the description in the newspaper clipping, I appeared to fit the bill perfectly. When we arrived and I saw nothing but tall, blond, skinny white women, I thought there must have been a major typo in the newspaper ad. The receptionist was cordial, yet cold. The look of disappointment on her face was meant to turn us away, but it didn't. However, the receptionist knew something else that would. She handed us a brochure to look at while we waited for someone to come out and speak with us. It was filled with pictures of big, gorgeous, busty women in the most beautiful clothes that I'd only seen on television. The brochure offered promises of opportunities to work for the world-renowned Ford Modeling agency or others like it. I was mesmerized by the details, and I sat there picturing myself on the runway somewhere in New York or Paris. That was until I got to the bottom of the brochure and my eyes became glued to the cost of the eight-week program – 800 dollars! What? That was exactly three months of school tuition for me and my three siblings. If I had thought Mom and Dad would agree to our sitting out of school for three months so I could become a famous model, I would have begged a little harder. But instead I grabbed my pale, pink satin jacket, adjusted my skin-tight lavender Gloria Vanderbilt pants and followed Mom out the door and down the hall to the elevator. From the corner of my eye, as we left, I saw a smirk of relief on the receptionist's face. We walked in silence. A part of me couldn't help feeling as if I was leaving my career on the runway behind.

Would this be my opportunity almost 10 years later? It wasn't modeling, but acting was close enough. If I walked out of the auditions, it wouldn't matter. Those people didn't know me. The worst

The Auditions

I always took the sure road, the safe road – and the boring road – in life.

that could happen was I'd walk away and never see them again. I searched my closet for the funkiest outfit I could find (in black, of course, because it's slimming). I touched up my makeup, fingered my hair and put on my only pair of black riding boots before heading out. This time I would take a chance. I would step out. What had playing it safe gotten me besides a dead-end job and a beautiful, empty apartment? I grabbed my purse and I was out the door. As I drove back through my canopy of colored leaves I thought of how I always took the sure road, the safe road – and the boring road – in life. It was time for me to add something different and less predictable. I needed a change and a little mystery.

TWO

Let's Dance

THINK ABOUT IT: *We see it all the time. People holding onto unhealthy relationships longer than they should. Why do we hang on to that which is clearly not good for us? Why is letting go so enormously hard to do? This especially seems to be the case for women. When we hold on to unhealthy relationships, it's because we've started to believe these relationships fill voids in our lives that no other relationships can fill. But rarely will your inner voice lead you down the wrong road. If you were driving down a street, looked up and saw a sign that said "wrong way," what would you do? You'd stop, turn the car around and go another direction. Why don't we listen to our inner voice when we reach the "stop" signs in our lives?*

.

It was late October. A cool, gentle breeze began to pick up as I walked quickly to the side door of the building. It was the first night of auditions. Not knowing where to go, I followed the few young ladies who entered before me. As we stepped inside, the long-haired, fair-skinned woman in front of me stuck her head through the doorway of an office asking, "Where do we go for auditions?"

"Downstairs through the kitchen and the first door on the left," a male voice replied. I assumed the male voice I heard belonged to the director, or at least someone who new about the play.

He told me what I needed to know. So, like a regular, I followed behind the others as they led the way. Oblivious to my presence behind them, they made small talk about who would probably show up and who wouldn't. It was already 7:30 and to my surprise, only a handful of people mingling in small groups of two or three had arrived. I casually smiled at the onlookers as I sat down in an empty seat halfway around the circle of chairs. For some reason, in my mind I had pictured a much bigger crowd. I had never been to the Kalamazoo Civic Theatre, but I had met a co-worker's husband, who was involved with the organization, at a dinner party. He encouraged me to audition, told me where I should go and who to ask for. With the added encouragement of my co-worker's telephone call, I decided, "Why not?" College life was over and Lord knows I needed a change that included some fun. I had lost touch with my few close friends when I joined a campus ministry three years earlier. I wasn't involved with much that made me feel confident about myself. So when this came along, I left the door wide open for possibilities.

When he walked into the room I knew he was the director. Not because his ability was so apparent, but his age and stature made him look out of place. In later years I heard someone else describe him as a man who "looks like a part-time, offbeat preacher." Instantly, I could feel his eyes staring at me. While trying to maintain an air of professionalism over the group, he prepared us for auditions. After completing the sign-in card, the process was simple. No outstanding acting talent here. Just regulars. People passing the time.

The social setting for an eclectic group of offbeat theatre groupies. My audition consisted of a few lines from a poem I wasn't familiar with, a few stanzas from a theatrical song and then I was done. That's it, nothing spectacular.

Afterwards, I hung around to do some people-watching. I mingled with a few of the regulars that lingered. It was a strange combination of people who'd come out for this audition. There was an older couple who looked out of place, but judging by the way they were received, they obviously were well-known professionals in the community. A big, broad boisterous woman sort of took over a major part of the auditions. Her skills and presence indicated that she had some experience on stage. Over in the corner, was a tall, loud-mouthed, skinny man who kept nothing but commotion going; and a short young man in his early twenties, who I'd seen on campus from time to time had little to say. A few more hopefuls stood out as shoo-ins, because their conversations led me to believe they had a personal relationship with the director. To make sure no one had one up on me, after putting on my coat and slinging my purse over my shoulder, I casually walked over to him and introduced myself.

"Hi, I'm LaShon. As I mentioned during the introductions, this is my first audition. When will we hear who makes the cut?"

"Umm, sometime next week I'll have them posted outside my office," he said with a slight, signifying smile. "I don't think you have anything to worry about."

As I said goodbye and left the theatre, I must have felt a dozen eyes following me across the pale-colored room until I reached the stairs. I was relieved, yet excited as I drove through the darkness back to my apartment. It had been a simple audition. I wondered if it was like that for people in Hollywood. My excitement grew, thinking about what was to come. To my surprise, I thought of the smile that came across the director's face when our eyes briefly met.

"Maybe it won't be so bad living here in Kalamazoo after all," I thought out loud to myself. That was the fall of 1990. It marked the beginning of a decade of challenges, changes and personal growth that would catapult me onto a course destined to change my life forever.

* * *

I could hear a voice saying, "Welcome to Hollywood!"

OK. Maybe not quite Hollywood, but it was the closest I'd ever get. After seeing my name on that list outside the director's door, I looked forward to the nightly rehearsals. They were a place for me to be different. I saw this as an opportunity for me to do something I had dreamed of doing since I was a little girl. I remember spending countless hours dreaming of being on television, starring in a sitcom with a role like the little girl Penny on "Good Times" or Dee on "What's Happening!" Not a realistic goal, maybe, for a little black girl from inner city Detroit. But this was real. It was my Hollywood. I began to feed on the excitement and energy that everyone brought with them to rehearsal, not to mention the fact that I would get to see him again: James McKay is what we'll call him. Why did this older man have me so intrigued? I don't know if I was more taken with him or more taken by his obvious interest in me. I could tell, even though it seemed like every available woman who came to that theatre wanted to get her hooks into him, he was sizing me up. I would catch him checking me out as if he was wondering, "What's her real story?"

"I've never seen you around here before," he said, striking up a conversation as we prepared to leave the theatre one evening. "You don't look like you are from Kalamazoo."

"I'm not," I nonchalantly replied. "I attended Western, graduated last year and just decided to stay."

Though I was casual in my response, I wondered why he made that statement. I talked differently than the locals and I did stand out, for some reason. In the past, this speech and composure had been a combination I didn't always appreciate, but this time it drew all the attention I wanted from James. I would linger around the "green room" after rehearsal, offering to help him clean up.

Our conversations would flow from one subject to another like a stream of running water with no end in sight.

It didn't take long before we found ourselves talking about things unrelated to theatre. I felt very comfortable chatting with him and I could tell he felt the same. Our conversations would flow from one subject to another like a stream of running water with no end in sight. James seemed to know so much about life. When he told me he was a minister preparing to become a pastor, I was caught off guard. It didn't fit with his personality. Something was missing from that match. I couldn't quite put my finger on it but somewhere in his character, the role of pastor seemed out of place. It didn't matter, though. Slowly and surely, seeing him became my primary reason for rushing home from work and off to rehearsal every evening.

After two months of five-night-a-week rehearsals, opening night had finally arrived. "Black Voices," a much-anticipated theatrical performance, was a huge success, receiving wonderful reviews. It opened the first Friday in February, just in time for Black History Month. It was like premiere night at the Apollo! Everyone who was anyone in the city came out, and we did not disappoint. "Black Voices" was not your traditional play, but a series of vignettes that included poetry, song, Negro spirituals and drama. Every night we performed to a sold-out crowd. My family even drove a few hours from Detroit to see it. The crowd was excited. And after the show, we were excited and ready to celebrate.

Everyone headed downtown to a popular nightspot. I toyed with the thought of going. The club scene had never been a favorite of mine, especially after I had accepted Christ three years earlier. So I usually avoided it. I weighed my options: sitting in front of the TV with popcorn and a Pepsi or hanging out and having fun with the group. I reasoned with myself. I had worked hard with them for the past two months. Didn't I deserve some fun, too?

I agreed to meet a friend at the club, but I told myself, "I don't drink, so I won't; I'll go, show my face, stay about an hour and make some excuse to leave." I tore up my walk-in closet trying to find something "club-appropriate" to wear. Since I hadn't been to a club in years, I had no idea what was fashionable. I picked a short black, "dressy" dress and black stockings, pulled my short hair up in my best version of a "French roll" and then set out for some fun. As I drove downtown, I thought about James and wondered if he would show up. The weather was unusually pleasant for February, so I didn't cringe when the wind blew through the ruffles of my short dress as I walked across the parking lot to the door of the club. I'd forgotten how dark nightclubs were. I could barely see as I peered through the crowd for a familiar face. I heard someone call out my name. I looked in that direction and saw members of the cast sitting in two booths in the center of the room, James included.

We all just kind of sat there, making small talk. The DJ played a nice variety of music. Out of nowhere, James asked me to dance. He caught me off guard. I wish I could remember what song was playing when we danced, but all I know is that it was a slow song. I was way too nervous to have even recognized it. He took my hand, led me to the dance floor and it seemed like the world stopped turning. "I don't slow dance all that well," I softly whispered in his ear. Instantly, I got a flashback of prom night and the disaster that had been when I tried to "social," as the slow dances were called then.

"It's OK, just follow my lead," his husky voice whispered back.

James pulled me close, and like smooth, creamy cake batter being poured into a pan, I slipped into his arms. In that moment, I was hooked. His touch, his smell, his body had me mesmerized like a school girl at her first high school dance. Before, I had mainly found him interesting because of his conversation. After our dance, I knew the passion between us had to be pursued and explored. A dance like that was meant to last forever.

* * *

"I'll call you when I get out of rehearsal, but it could be a long one tonight," he told me. We were now a few months into our courtship, and I shared James' time with his ongoing commitment to rehearsals at the theatre.

"If it's too late, I'll catch up with you tomorrow," I answered. "Maybe we can do lunch if you have the time."

"Will do. Talk with you tomorrow."

Hmmm. Another long night, I thought. I knew rehearsal didn't end until 9 and that meant more like 9:40 or 10 for the director. Seemed like these long rehearsals were becoming the norm, not the exception. I'd spent a fair amount of time in James' rehearsals and usually, they could have ended a lot sooner than they did.

I felt the theatre had become somewhat off-limits to me once we started dating. He discouraged my being there. At first, it struck me as kind of odd that he didn't want me around the theatre, since this was the very thing that brought us together. I also had my concerns because I knew the groupie type of women who hung around the place. But I pretended it didn't matter and threw myself into my classes. Yes, I was back in school working on a graduate degree. Trying to maintain a rigorous schedule as a student in the evening and, of course, working my full-time job during the day kept me busy. I didn't miss the long hours that went along with theatre rehearsal.

James and I quickly settled into a routine of late-night phone calls, or dinners and movies when his schedule allowed. Timeliness wasn't his strong point. Some-

I continuously ignored the signs that something wasn't quite right.

times I wouldn't hear from him for days, and when I did it could be well after 11 at night. As time went on, I continuously ignored the signs that something wasn't quite right. My rationale? Having someone sometimes was better than having no one all the time. So I settled for his questionable disappearances and inconsistent behavior.

But eventually my patience wore thin. Over the next year or so we went through a series of breakups and on-again/off-again periods. There was a bad sign that I clearly ignored during the "on-again" days. The more time we spent together, the more I realized how different we were, and that we didn't belong together as a couple. I'm certain our eleven-and-a-half-year age difference played a major role in complicating matters. He was settled in areas of his life where I was just establishing myself. He was focused on long-term goals, while I was still exploring possibilities. We were worlds apart in our life experiences. I lived a sheltered childhood, and college was my first experience away from home. Being away from the protective wings of my parents during my freshman year was a welcomed eye-opener for me. I took advantage of the ability to make my own decisions. Some good, some bad. But even during college, halfway through my junior year I fell back on what was familiar. I joined a campus ministry that wrapped its arms around me so tightly I rarely had to think for myself. My experiences with men were close to non-existent. While I was still trying to find my way, James was

> *I took advantage of the ability to my my own decisions.*

already well on his. He had been married, divorced, fired from a job and was moving further into a second career when we met. He never told me he had been married. A mutual friend let it slip. When I questioned him about it, he quickly explained it away. From what he did say, I knew there was history beyond their short-lived union. They stayed in touch after their split and even communicated regularly. I found that to be rather odd, given that there were no children between them and there was no real reason for them to remain in each others' lives. James left a lot unsaid and he left me feeling uncertain. As all this became clear to me, I struggled with how to make it work, to make it fit into my life.

My spirit was leading me in a different direction, but I had my own agenda.

Being with James didn't give me the security I thought it would and should have. It actually made me feel insecure and uncertain. It was no secret that many female eyes had been on him prior to my arrival. Some of them made it known that my presence was an intrusion. These weren't just any old theatre groupies, but close friends of his, even board members with the theatre, who would've preferred I just go back to wherever I'd come from. He and I argued all the time about their disrespect toward me and his inability to recognize or address it. He knew the truth, whether he admitted it or not.

My spirit was leading me in a different direction, but I had my own agenda. I endured months of late-night get-togethers and occasionally seeing him on the weekends. But even when he was there, it was as if...he wasn't.

For some reason neither of us would walk away and call it quits – for good. We continued in this rollercoaster relationship for the next two years.

Three

Oh Boy! A Wedding!

THINK ABOUT IT: *If you are trying to make your relationship work, like forcing a square cube into a round hole, obviously it's not going to be a good fit. And the worst thing you can do is gamble on a commitment as serious as marriage being the solution to your problems, rather than the ultimate sign of love for your partner. There's a word to describe most people who marry for appearances or circumstances outside their relationship: divorced. Listen to your inner voice before making the commitment to marry, especially if you're considering a second time. Many of us identify that "inner voice" with God. If we don't trust ourselves, we can certainly trust the voice of the Creator. He will never lead us down the wrong path.*

I couldn't figure it out! My stomach never felt so queasy. The sight and smell of food literally made me sick. When lunchtime rolled around at work, I'd make excuses for not going to lunch with the ladies in the office. Usually, lunch hour was my favorite part of the work day, as it meant a break from the awful job that I still loathed. Now it was a time for avoiding others. "I'm meeting James for dinner," I would say, "gotta save my appetite."

Truth was the smell of any food made me feel nauseated. My

A zillion and one thoughts went through my head.

stomach dropped to my knees as my mind contemplated the possibility that I might be preg-...

"Of course you are," Traniece, my best friend, told me.

"I am not pregnant," I told her.

"Well, you tell me why your 'monthly visitor' is four days late, you haven't eaten in days because you can't stand the sight of food and you feel nauseated."

I hated to admit it, but she was right...I thought. I didn't know. I didn't want to think about it! Yes, James and I were back together. We were even talking about getting married the following fall, but a baby was nothing I had in mind. A zillion and one thoughts went through my head. Everything from how I really and truly felt about him to my family, to motherhood and a pre-marital pregnancy.

How did I let this happen? This isn't how it was supposed to go for me. I did everything the right way. By the book. What would I do if...Traniece was right?

Annoyed with her constant urging, I hesitantly got up and drove a half mile to Perry Drugs. I wandered around the store, up and down the aisles until I got the nerve to go down the one marked "feminine hygiene." I stood there reading the entire directions – every word on the box – before settling on an over-the-counter pregnancy test. I had to know. Late that night, locked away by myself in the little bathroom of my apartment, I took the test. The 15-minute wait felt like a lifetime. I read and re-read the directions over and over again trying to pass time. A "minus" sign if I wasn't, or a pink "plus" sign if I was would tell me what I needed to know. I sat there waiting, and waiting, and waiting. I was so deep in thought that I didn't realize 25 minutes had gone by. When I got up the nerve, I picked up the test from the edge of the sink and just stared at the stick. It was pink! Bright pink! Fuchsia pink! I was pregnant.

Sick as could be, the next morning I pulled myself out of the bed and went to the office. It was Friday. One more day and then I would have the whole weekend to discuss this with James. I called him from work to let him know how I was feeling. "Meet me at my apartment at 5," I told him. "I've been having this terrible shortness of breath, like my heart is skipping a beat off and on all week. I think I need to see a doctor."

"You think you need to go to the doctor for shortness of breath?" he asked.

My quiet pause let him know I didn't like his response.

He followed up with a more appropriate question.

"What do you think it is?"

"I don't know. I've never had this funny feeling before. I need to talk to you about something else anyway. It's important."

I was home when he arrived. I wanted to clear my mind before seeing him. I knew I had to at least give him a heads up before we went to the doctor's office. We made the ride to Westwood Family Medical Center mostly in silence. Once we pulled up, I stopped him before he could get out. I spilled everything: the test results, my concerns about us. Everything. Surprisingly, he didn't have much of a reply. But that didn't make me feel any better. "Let's see what the doctor has to say before we make any rash decisions or jump to any conclusions," was his only response.

I wasn't in any position to agree or disagree about his level of excitement. About an hour later, it was confirmed. I was definitely pregnant. We stood outside the clinic and hugged under the dim sunlight as it faded behind rays from a beautiful rainbow in the sky. The fresh smell of rain was in the air and, despite the unsettling news we'd just received, I felt safe and secure in his arms. Everything was going to be alright.

It had to be.

*　*　*

My dreams were beginning to come true. I was about to get married. And to a man being groomed as a pastor on his way to leading a church. Sure it was a little sooner than expected, but what was wrong with moving our wedding plans ahead 10 months? I spent the next several weeks planning my big day. The usual business that comes with planning a wedding was intensified by our already overwhelming schedules. Between his late-night rehearsals at the theatre, his church responsibilities and my graduate classes and job, we had to schedule a meeting just to confirm the date. After days of crunching the calendar we settled on November 21st.

The church we chose in Detroit was beautiful. It was the one I'd grown up in. Even as early as August, we could see color on the tips of the tree leaves beginning to change around the half-block-long church. The sun gleamed and glistened as we pulled into the nearly empty parking lot. By November this would make a beautiful backdrop for the outdoor pictures of our wedding party. Today, it's still one of the most beautiful churches in the city. I had always known I'd get married there. As a little girl, I dreamed of walking down the long aisle of red carpet lined with rich Maplewood pews. It was an old church, yet it had a warm and modern feel. The altar where we would stand and exchange our vows was wide and deep. Simple, but elegant. I remember how I would daydream with such excitement and anticipation, imagining the pastor's words, "I now present to you Rev. and Mrs. ..."

"Are you getting out?" a voice called, interrupting my daydream. "LaShon, we're here. Are you getting out?"

I was just short of a million miles away, when James asked the question.

"I thought we were going to stop by my Mom's and Dad's first," I said, grabbing my purse and taking two steps to catch up with him.

"We'll see them afterwards," he said.

We were late. Pastor Wixmon had been expecting us for an hour. It was like a mini-reunion. Over the past seven years, I'd seen Pastor Wixmon only during my occasional visits home from Kalamazoo. I hadn't been back to visit in quite a while. My surprise was the greeting between the pastor and James. Like long, lost buddies, they engaged in conversation I knew nothing about. As it turns out, they were connected through a mutual friend, a Lutheran pastor who I wouldn't meet until the wedding day. They were all connected through the Black Ministry Lutheran Convocation, an annual conference that brought all black Lutherans together.

Having discussed the details, as we said our goodbyes, I agreed to keep Pastor Wixmon posted on any plans and changes prior to the rehearsal dinner, which would be held in the church's fellowship hall. I spent the remainder of the weekend with my parents, who lived less than a block from the church. Meanwhile, James visited his relatives and friends. After college he'd moved to the Detroit area and even taught in the public school system before taking the theatre job and moving back to Kalamazoo. It was during this time in Detroit that he began his pastoral training.

Looking back, we did consider our decision to get married carefully. Even though our relationship had seen its share of ups and downs, we agreed that marriage was what we both wanted. But I honestly questioned whether things would've turned out differently, had the baby not been a concern. Even while planning a rushed wedding, we didn't seem to be on the same page. Nothing changed with James' distant, evasive behavior. Are men just different? I wondered. Do the details of what should be the happiest day of their lives mean so little to them? It had become my habit, so I just continued to ignore the lingering signs that not even a pregnancy should be reason enough for this wedding to take place. I didn't have time to dwell on the minor problems that nagged at me. I had bigger priorities like going to class, working full-time and, now single-handedly planning a wedding.

When the day finally arrived, my five bridesmaids and two junior bridesmaids were elegantly draped in emerald green and black velvet dresses trimmed in gold. They looked like beautiful black goddesses next to the handsomely dressed groomsmen decked out in Michael Jordan-brand tuxedos. Set to start promptly at 4, the candlelight evening ceremony was delayed by a University of Michigan football game that was still in its fourth quarter! I couldn't believe it! The guys – groom included – were huddled up in front of a small color TV in the fellowship hall trying to catch the last few minutes.

> *What my parents thought and, honestly, what everyone else thought was important to me.*

    Eventually, things got underway. For a brief moment I saw the trickle of a tear starting in my Dad's eye as he reached out to take my arm at the bottom of the stairs. I hesitated and looked at him for any last-minute words of wisdom. I wanted him to tell me everything would be alright, or to say I shouldn't do it if I had doubts. I wanted him to assure me that the happiness of the moment would last forever. He only smiled, asked if I was OK and walked me to the doorway of the sanctuary where everyone was waiting. I wanted to make him proud of me. What my parents thought and, honestly, what everyone else thought was important to me. It was that type of misguided thinking that kept me from doing things based on my own feelings. That kept me from growing as an adult.

    But this was my wedding day. All these people were here for me. Looking at me. This was my day to be happy. It seemed like it took forever to walk down the aisle. As I got closer, for some reason I began to cry. Out of joy or something else, I still don't know. I just cried. When I was close enough to James and my eyes met his, they were warm and comforting. He took my arm from my father and wrapped it in his own as we walked together to the altar. Together forever. For always...

* * *

The closest I ever felt to him was on our wedding night. Not a real honeymoon. Just a few nights stay in a beautifully decorated hotel suite. It was a young bride's dream, fulfilling my every expectation. Is this what marriage did for two people in love? Did pledging commitment to each other in front of 200 onlookers bring out their true feelings for one another? I could get used to this really fast.

But our focus soon moved from wedding bliss to preparing for the arrival of a new baby. Moving two full apartments of furniture into one living space was a feat in and of itself. My belly was in full bloom and my body was trying to get used to the extra 15 pounds it was carrying. Meanwhile, I had never found the time to look for another job, so I was moving into my fourth year at the same place where my sentiments hadn't changed since day one. Overwhelmed wasn't a strong enough description for what I was beginning to feel. The changes were just too much. Something had to give before I broke. Reluctantly, I took a semester off from school to catch my breath – which, by the way, was still showing signs of shortness, even after my doctor's visit.

My final month of pregnancy consisted of sleep and eating, but mostly sleep. That's it. Nothing else. Now at least twenty pounds heavier, I was having issues with my weight and the doctor wanted me off my feet. This left very little room for quality time between James and me. But it made things easier for him, since he had little time anyway between his church and theatre duties. Something always seemed to keep him out of the house. Away from home.

Then one day something was different. On a Friday, I woke up full of energy, something I'd lacked since about five months earlier. Ready to clean everything in sight, I puttered around our home like a housekeeper on her first day at work. Thank God for a popular mega-grocery chain that stayed open 24 hours. Shortly after midnight, I was up and down the aisles buying enough food to feed a family of six.

"Just come and go with me. I won't be long," I had said to my husband.

James wasn't budging.

"It's 12 o'clock in the morning, LaShon. I'm not going grocery shopping. Whatever we need can wait until tomorrow."

It was a good thing I didn't take his advice. My Saturday morning began with the worst pain I've ever felt. Paralyzed, I lay there motionless. I held my breath, fearful that any more movement might intensify the sharp, piercing pain in the bottom of my stomach. Just as I exhaled it hit me again. This time I recognized what it was. The baby book I'd been reading in between my seemingly month-long naps described labor as sharp pains that felt like cramps. I sat up in the bed and announced, "I'm going into labor."

* * *

We had a beautiful baby boy! After a day and a half of excruciating labor we were the proud parents of a 7-pound, 21-inch bundle of joy. My wedding day was quickly replaced with the date of April 25, 1993 as the happiest of my life. Nothing compares to the joy of having a child. For a moment, it did bring my husband and I closer, but it also presented its own unique set of challenges as I showed signs of postpartum depression. It didn't take long before James was back to his old habits of short days at home and long nights at the theatre.

FOUR

Everything In Between

THINK ABOUT IT: *Moments of reflection can serve a much greater purpose than creating space for temporary, passing thoughts.* A walk in the garden, a drive down a quiet road, or even a quick coffee break during work hours can all provide opportunities to gain clarity about the issues we face. Whether it's relationship trouble or another concern, focusing on possible answers brings us closer to solutions. Spend moments of reflection objectively asking yourself questions like, "How did I reach this point?", "Why did I make that decision?" and "What will it take to correct my problem?" Seems simple enough, but too often we let our minds wander so much that we only end up stressing ourselves even more. Have you spent some time in quiet reflection today?

A warm cup of chamomile tea and honey was the perfect end to what had been a hectic week. Cramming for end-of-semester exams, interviewing prospects for home childcare providers and the never-ending meetings at church, my sorority and work had stretched me beyond exhaustion. What I would've given for a real vacation on a beach in sunny Jamaica! But daydreaming with tea and honey was about all I had time for. No one was up yet, so I stole a few moments of serenity on the second-story balcony of our townhouse and exhaled. The Channel 3 weather guy had promised a summer-like day. My thoughts turned again, as they had several times during the past week, toward the possibility of taking another semester off from school. I'd been going non-stop since Jay was born, sometimes trying to function on as little as six hours of interrupted sleep. My fear was that if I stopped going to class again I wouldn't finish. I'd come too far to stop. Between sips of tea, my mind raced with concerns about all that was going on in my life. I constantly had the feeling that I was forgetting something, that things were being left undone. Like strapping on a seatbelt, I forced myself not to jump up and attend to the many things I told myself I should be doing, instead of what I was handling at the moment. I also thought about how little time James and I spent together those past few months. Since the theatre took a break during the summer, I was looking forward to some much-needed attention from my husband. I closed my eyes and listened to my neighbor stirring around in her kitchen next door as she prepared a late breakfast. Startled by my phone ringing, I knew everyone in our house would soon be awake.

    James and I answered the phone at the same time, so he hung up after saying hello to my father. Mom or Dad called every Saturday. Actually, we talked nearly every day. We all did, including my three siblings. Between us, we kept AT&T in business and their stock prices on the upswing. At one point when I was in college, all of us were living in different cities or states, using Dad's calling card to pay for our communication. It only took one month of a $1,000 phone bill for him to put an end to that.

"Are you up yet? How's my grandson," Dad asked me.

"I'm fine, thank you for asking, and hopefully he is still sleeping," I said. "What's going on there?"

There was always something going on. He would bring me up to date on my sisters and brother. It was usually yesterday's news, as one or the other of my siblings had already beaten him to the punch. Dad felt it was his place to track the business of all of us, everyone, even our neighbors. The neighbors must have agreed, since most of them came to him for advice on something or another. While we chatted, Mom was in the kitchen preparing his favorite breakfast, salmon croquettes, rice and biscuits. She hadn't been able to make the adjustment from cooking for six to just two, so they were sure to have the same meal for lunch.

"We thought about taking a drive that way later today, if you all were going to be around," Dad said.

"That sounds good. James is still asleep. Let me talk to him and get back with you."

Dad had been sick the last few times I talked to him. I wasn't sure if I wanted him on the road all day. Never one to complain, he'd been to the doctor more than usual over the past few months.

As I contemplated his health and his proposed visit, I heard footsteps coming down the stairs. James and little Jay were up. My siesta was over.

* * *

As quickly as it had arrived, summer was gone. I actually found myself becoming jealous and resentful of James' time at the theatre. The long hours, the people, the environment. We hadn't even spent that extra time together that I hoped for when the theatre went on its summer hiatus. What had already been a sore spot during our courtship was now a strain on our young marriage. And I had good reason to feel the way I did. It wasn't a secret how some of the people James associated with felt about me. They openly showed their dislike whenever I came around. This caused him to push me away from his activities even more than before. He would try and convince me to believe the issue was my own insecurity. He knew he had to make a choice, but refused. Instead, he continued to allow, and even embrace, the position his conflict between work and our relationship left him in. We argued constantly.

> *I felt like I had nowhere to turn. Life for me became a series of going through the motions.*

We desperately needed the counseling he often provided to couples at the church. If he wasn't at the theatre, he was helping congregation members, attending a meeting or working on a sermon. I felt like I had nowhere to turn. Life for me became a series of going through the motions. It didn't take long before I began wondering if I had made a huge mistake.

James was comfortable in his double life. By day and night he was a theatre director, setting few boundaries for his actors and actresses, who tolerated some of everything from their leader. On Sunday morning he was a preacher, quoting scriptures that was hard to find evidence of his believing when he was outside of church.

Who would counsel me? I was the pastor's wife. Would I go to the members? To the other pastors? Even if I did, I couldn't help feeling as if nothing would be said or done. I saw signs of compromise in the character of leaders all the way up this church's hierarchy. It was as if my only choice was to accept things as they were. That was like having no choice at all.

Five

True Confessions

THINK ABOUT IT: *Very seldom do behavior patterns mean anything other than what they appear to mean. A person who is hiding something will usually show, through actions, that he or she has something to hide. This is especially the case in marriages where dishonesty is a factor. But why do we kick and beat ourselves for giving trust to our ex after the marriage ends? You're supposed to trust your husband. You should be surprised when your wife lies to you. If you think dishonesty from a mate comes with the territory, you've married the wrong person. Rather than hating yourself because you gave a spouse the benefit of the doubt, always remember that he or she is the only person who has reason to be ashamed.*

It was Valentine's Day weekend and we were headed to Detroit where the wedding of my husband's college roommate was to take place. "Perfect!" I thought. This would do us both some good, since it had been a rough holiday season a few months before. We drove the next two hours mostly in silence with only the whining and noises of our 22-month-old as background. An impromptu visit from Mrs. Webber one Sunday before Christmas in 1995 popped into my mind. The Webbers were our son's surrogate godparents.

I wasn't much of a coffee drinker at that time, but I poured myself a cup and sat it down on the small end table next to hers. James had sat across from us, nervously. He looked as if he was bracing himself for some bad news, but kept silent. A faithful, loyal, longtime church member, Mrs. Webber was one of the few ladies who truly embraced me when I joined the church after James and I married. She adored Jay, and every Thursday evening I counted on her to baby-sit while I attended class.

We talked a bit about church service and our holiday plans, but she was clearly distracted. The tone in her voice was distant and shallow. She was searching for the right words to say. Some turn in the conversation's direction to help her share what she really wanted to tell me. She never found the right moment, so she just jumped right in.

I was shocked by what she said.

Her husband had fathered a child outside their marriage. The image of Mr. Webber wouldn't leave my mind. He was quiet and reserved. Man, an ideal spouse. He'd lost most of his speech due to a stroke a few years earlier, but he often communicated with his big, wide eyes and infectious smile. When he felt comfortable enough with you to attempt a conversation, Mrs. Webber would always be right there to finish his thoughts, or to help guide the conversation so he didn't have to say too much. To me they were the perfect married couple.

He just didn't seem like the kind of man who would do such a thing. Not only another woman, but a child too? What was he thinking? What was he looking for? He had the whole package at home. Weren't his wife's beauty and great personality enough? Mrs. Webber was a lovely, fair-complexioned, thin and very well-kept lady, who somewhat resembled Lena Horne. Beautiful inside and out. At first she might come across as a bit overbearing, but all around, she was a nice, happy-go-lucky person.

James said nothing. He sat sternly and listened. I didn't know what to say. I'd known her now for three-plus years, attended the same church, saw her every Thursday and had dinner with her at least once a month, but she had never as much as hinted about this...until now.

Why was this so important after three years of friendship that it couldn't have waited until another time?

"Now?" I thought. Why was she telling us this now?

It wasn't a babysitting day, and she had just showed up unannounced and uninvited on a Sunday afternoon. Why was this so important after three years of friendship that it couldn't have waited until another time?

I had a slew of questions which I tried to ask tactfully. I couldn't help wondering why she stayed with her husband. How did they manage to keep it all a secret from their daughter for more than a dozen years? I really wanted to know much more, but felt that maybe I didn't know her well enough to ask such personal questions. I politely refilled her cup of coffee since she made no moves toward the front door.

It was our turn to speak, so Mrs. Webber sat there waiting as if she had some other secret that was related to what she had just revealed – like a junior high school girl who had shared her most embarrassing diary entry, in the hopes that her friend would do the same. Besides the turbulent road our relationship had been traveling in recent months – which wasn't completely out of the ordinary for any young marriage – I had nothing to share. I smiled a polite, uncomfortable smile and sipped my lukewarm coffee. We both glanced at Jay playing with his building blocks on the floor and waited. James never said a word. He sat in his chair, looking straight ahead. Silent. But now I could hear him speaking.

"We're stuck in traffic," he said staring at the road in front of us.

"What?"

"I said I wonder how long we are going to be stuck in traffic," he repeated.

Having brought my mind back to the present, I realized it was probably the most he had said to me since we got on the road to Detroit.

"Oh, I don't know," I said. "I'm looking forward to Tyrone's wedding. Where did you say they met?"

"At church in Grand Rapids. I didn't know you were planning on going. I thought you would stay with Jay at your parents'."

"Why would I do that? Why wouldn't I go to the wedding? You're in the wedding."

"I'm in the wedding. Not you."

I looked at him as if he were crazy! Why should I not attend this event with my husband? Stuck in traffic now, he had nowhere to go and no way to divert his attention from the question.

"I'm going to the wedding!"

Here I was thinking this whole weekend might be just what we needed after all his unusual behavior and late-night disappearing acts. Maybe it would remind us – actually him – of our love, vows and commitment to each other and why we got married. I couldn't have been more wrong.

And James couldn't have been more right! I should have stayed at home. The weekend was a disaster. He avoided me all night long at the wedding and reception. We did nothing together, not even dance. He ignored me the entire time, and his friends practically did the same. Their behavior toward me was on a level I had never experienced. We came back from the wedding in the same state of disrepair as when we'd left home. No matter what I said or did, nothing was improving. His disappearing acts began to increase to three or four times a week.

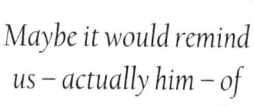

> *Maybe it would remind us – actually him – of our love, vows and commitment to each other and why we got married.*

Later, on another weekend trip he took by himself to Gary, Indiana for a visit with his mother, and supposedly to hang out with some fraternity buddies, I wound up calling the police and nearly filing a missing person report. When he left that Friday evening for Indiana all I knew was where he would be staying.

"Why can't Jay and I go?" I asked. "Your mom would love to see Jay."

"I need some time to think, be by myself," he answered. "I'll call you when I get there."

Although he'd been acting even more suspiciously, I never imagined there was anything more to his trip than what he told me. So he left and we stayed at home.

When he didn't call, I called his mother. She was surprised to hear my voice: "Did James make it okay? He was supposed to call when he got to your house and he hasn't called."

"Ohhh...James is not here," she said, puzzled.

"Umm...do you know if he is staying at Sandra's?" I asked, referring to his sister.

"Yeah, maybe he is."

"Well can you have him call me if he happens to come there?"

We talked a few more minutes about her grandson Jay, who she adored, and then we hung up. I could never remember Sandra's number, but after several attempts I finally got a familiar "Hello."

"Hi, Sandra. Have you heard from James?"

"Noooo," was her reply.

"Well, he left here around 7 headed that way to meet a few fraternity brothers and said he would check in with you or your mom. Did he tell you he was coming?"

"Noooo," again was her puzzled reply.

I wondered to myself, "What the hell is her problem?"

"Wellllll," I said, stretching my syllable like she had, "please tell him to call me when he gets there."

Before she could ask about Jay, I abruptly hung up the phone. She was hiding something.

After Jay fell asleep around 11, I went back downstairs to watch a little more TV. It was really just something for me to keep my mind off James. About an hour later, I woke up to find the TV watching me. It was after midnight! Feeling a little panicky, I thought about calling his mother again, but I called mine instead. Thank God Dad answered the phone. It was always good to hear his voice. Even as a grown, married woman, I found comfort in talking to Dad.

"He probably just forgot to call. He'll call in the morning," my father said.

I took Dad's advice and went upstairs to bed, adding a little more of my own optimism: "He'll probably call right after I fall asleep."

Like clockwork, Jay, now 2 years old, woke me up around 7 a.m. Not yet fully awake, I jumped when I realized it was morning and James still hadn't called all night. After breakfast I couldn't wait any longer and called his mother again. She'd not heard a word from him. Nothing. I alternated calls between his family and mine all day long. I was worried out of my mind. By around 11 that night I felt I had no other choice than to contact the police. This seemed to get a reaction from James' sister, and she convinced me to wait until morning since he was due home on Sunday anyway. Reluctantly, I did. Going to church that morning was out of the question. I wasn't leaving the house until I heard from him.

Sunday arrived and I'd done all the waiting I was going to do. I gave a telephone operator all of my husband's information. While waiting for the police to show, I called his sister again and told her what I had done.

There was a knock at the door the same time my phone rang with the call I'd been waiting on. As I picked it up, I peered through the peep hole and hollered, "Just a minute, please" to the two officers outside.

"Hello," I said into the phone.

"LaShon, what's going on?"

"James? Where are you? Are you okay? I've been calling everywhere for the past two days and no one knew where you were. The police... I called the police!"

"I know. You didn't have to call the police."

"Well you didn't call and no one heard from you."

"I'm OK. Just call them back and tell them I'm OK."

"It's too late. They're at the door now. Why didn't you call me?"

"Go to the door and tell them you've talked to me and I'm OK."

"Why didn't you call me?" I asked again.

He could hear them knocking outside.

"LaShon, answer the door!"

I walked across the hallway with the phone in my hand and answered.

"Hello, are you Mrs. McKay?" the officers asked.

"Yes."

"We got a call to this address about your husband missing."

A long silence, then...

"Did you call about your husband missing?"

"Umm, yes."

"Well can we come in? We need to ask you some questions."

I heard James on the other end of the phone telling me to let the police know they could leave.

"Well, this is my husband on the phone and he says he is OK."

"Are you sure that is your husband?"

Now I was looking at them like they were crazy. Was I sure? I knew what my husband sounded like!

"Yes, I'm sure. Officer, I apologize if I caused any problems but he called just before you arrived and I only called because I hadn't heard from him in two days."

"We will have to take down some information," they said.

I finished up with the officers. They seemed quite disturbed that I had inconvenienced them.

Both relieved and angry, I told James I would see him when he got home. I hung up.

In less than two hours he was coming through the door. The more and more he talked, the more flimsy his excuse for not calling seemed. I had my doubts. He knew it, too. Well, my doubts turned out to be valid. Months later, I found out he had never left the city in the first place. Even after that episode, his disappearing acts continued.

> *He'd made the decision to shut himself down and shut me out.*

Ultimately, I couldn't take it anymore. I blew up, mostly because I didn't understand where this behavior was coming from. He'd made the decision to shut himself down and shut me out.

I'd had enough. One morning I took Jay to daycare, skipped work and announced that I would be back home. We had to talk. Apparently, he had been expecting this because he didn't try and avoid the conversation, for a change. He was ready to talk as much as I was.

Without coaxing, he started the conversation and I couldn't believe the first thing that came out of his mouth. With little warning, he began, "I don't love you anymore and we have to get a divorce. One of my board members has an apartment in the back of his house and I will be moving at the end of the month. At best we can see what happens in a few months, but at worst..." He had this contentious tone in his voice that made me want to puke.

I sat on our white loveseat with him across the room on the matching sofa. He stared at me with a look in his eyes I had never seen before. There was something about that piercing glare I couldn't quite make out. Who was this strange man in my home, posing and impersonating my husband? What had he done with James? Did he just say "divorce?" Where was this coming from?

My heart dropped into my stomach like a 20-pound bowling ball. His words cut my heart like a knife cutting cheese. An enormous aching pain pierced the back of my neck and continued down the middle of my back. I just sat there numb. The only movement from me was the roll of tears down my face and into the palms of my hands. I spent the entire day on that white loveseat. Crying my eyes out.

The next few days turned into weeks of the same thing: James staying at work late, sleeping downstairs in the living room and having very little to say to me. When he did speak, it was only to tell one lie after another. I didn't know what to think. Nothing I said or did mattered anyway. I convinced myself he was going through some male midlife crisis and would soon come to his senses. Things would get back to normal. But what was normal?

Each day I'd come home from work wondering if he would be there, hoping and praying he wouldn't leave. Yet, a part of me wanted him to go. My wanting him there wasn't because of my inability to care for myself and my child, although I did have anxious thoughts about how I could do this. I simply deserved better than having a man walk out on me. I was afraid of being alone, afraid of losing the family I had longed for all my life: a husband, kids and a suburban house. My picture-perfect family was disappearing, and the emptiness I felt in the weeks and years to come was a pain that took too long to get over.

James did finally leave...four days before my 29th birthday.

Six

The Beginning of the End

THINK ABOUT IT: *Have you ever tried to pray and found that no words would come out? If so, try writing your thoughts to God, to the universe, to yourself. It's a way of dealing with this sudden-death experience called divorce, a way to empty out everything bottled up inside you, especially when you've been unable to communicate with your spouse. It doesn't have to be perfect grammar or spelling, and it doesn't have to be poetic. But writing can give you the strength needed to cope from day to day. With friends and family you can't always divulge your most private, personal thoughts for fear of being judged, or even receiving biased support and feedback. However, in a private journal, you're free to "tell all," no matter what, while walking closer and closer to peace and truth. It's also a way of regaining your sense of control. By organizing your thoughts on paper, you can re-focus and re-center yourself after an experience that may have left you feeling helpless.*

The day I was served with divorce papers had to have been the longest 24 hours of my life. It was early May 1996. Jay and I had just moved out of the townhouse into a two-bedroom, lower-level apartment. That day, I wasn't prepared for the knock at the door. Once I answered, a courier shoved the papers into my hand and was departing up the short flight of stairs and through the double doors of our building before I knew what was happening. After reading the papers, my legs nearly gave out from beneath me, but I managed to guide my fall into a chair inches away from the front door. It was now official. We were getting divorced. I stared at the paperwork in disbelief. A powerful surge of emotion came over me. Anger, sadness and fear were all rolled up in one, but mostly anger. Yeah, I was angry. Just who did he think he was, divorcing me? I quickly grew even more outraged as what was happening finally began to sink in. I sat there on the edge of my chair, desperately trying to wake up from this awful nightmare – only to realize I was wide awake and this wasn't a dream. How did we get to this point? How did I get to this place in my 29 short years?

My mind drifted back to a few months before we were married. I recalled the events as if they had happened only last week. Like most couples, we had a rough first year or so while getting to know one another, but nothing transpired to signal a divorce in our future. Maybe I had ignored too many signs early on, before we were married. As I thought about it, the signs actually read like neon, flashing letters. The funny thing is I thought I was hearing from God. I distinctly remember driving through downtown Kalamazoo one Sunday, thinking about how nice it would be to make my road trips home to Detroit with a husband in tow. That's when I heard God speak to me about marrying James. I would have pulled my car over if it had not been for the young teenager riding my bumper. Judging by the way he cut his eyes at me when he rushed past, I must have slowed down during my daydream without realizing it. But the thoughts were real and vivid; I remember them to this day. God told me I was going to have a husband. OK, maybe He didn't actually say it would be James, but who else was there? We were dating and he was a pastor in training; he fit the bill perfectly. So I thought...

As I reflected on all this history between us, Jay's soft little touch to my thigh brought me back to reality. I looked down to find these gorgeous, big brown eyes looking up at me. Jay maneuvered my hands out of his way and climbed into my lap. He had been in his room playing, which was a good thing. I had promised myself there would be no more tears in front of him. He had seen mommy cry more than he needed to already.

"You must be hungry," I said. "Mommy is hungry, too."

After turning on the Disney Channel for him I headed to the kitchen.

While standing over the sink repeatedly rewashing the same juice glass, I was overcome with emotion again. This time it was a sadness far beyond my control. Was this really happening? I turned on the water to help drown out the sound of my crying so Jay wouldn't hear me.

How many more lies, disappointments and broken promises would I have to endure? Holidays and anniversaries were never going to be the same, not to mention birthdays. This had already become a reality for me, having realized these things the day James moved out.

On that day, Jay and I had entered the narrow hallway of the old townhouse and immediately I knew something was different. There was an airy, empty feeling. I dismissed it, took off our coats, picked

The Beginning of the End

up Jay and walked into the living room.

I froze!

I stood there thinking that I must have walked into the wrong apartment, but then remembered that my keys had already opened the door. An empty space remained where the large, black leather recliner used to be. It had been an early Christmas gift for James. The CD/stereo player was gone and other minor items were also missing. Jay scrambled out of my arms as I turned to walk back through the hallway. I took note of things that had disappeared from the kitchen and dining area. I began to go through the house wondering when he had time to remove all this. The previous night when he didn't come home until the early morning hours, I didn't have the energy to engage in another routine argument. When I'd left for work that morning I had no idea he would be spending the day moving out unannounced. I sat on the edge of our bed in disbelief. My eyes wandered around the room and became fixated on the walk-in closet. His side of the walk-in, empty: Shoes, shirts, ties, pants – everything was gone. It took him days to move all this junk into the house, but miraculously, he was able to move it out in fewer than eight hours.

I heard a weary little voice from the bottom of the stairs. Those big brown eyes actually put a grin on my face until I carried Jay down to the basement. James must have run out of time because

When I'd left for work that morning I had no idea he would be spending the day moving out unannounced.

The Beginning of the End

the majority of his junk down there hadn't been touched. I thought about Angela Bassett's clothes – burning – fire scene in the movie "Waiting to Exhale" after her cheating husband announced his leaving her for another woman. How satisfying it would be to set all his stuff on fire. My luck, it would back fire on me as we had no home owners or rental insurance. This meant he would be back. Still in disbelief, my eyes just roamed around the room.

I heard the key turn in the door and, like lightning, Jay and I beat it back up the stairs. I had a few choice words for James.

"So this is how you plan to do it? Just move out in the middle of the day while I'm at work?" I demanded.

Trying to sound sympathetic, he said, "LaShon, I told you weeks ago I was leaving."

"Yeah, well you also told me years ago, 'For better or for worse.' Obviously, I shouldn't have believed that."

"I just think a little time apart will give us some clarity."

"Clarity for whom, James?" I asked. "I don't need clarity. I'm not the one confused."

"We have to get a divorce," was his response again.

"Well which one is it, James? If you need clarity, why do we have to get a divorce?"

I didn't even wait for an answer. I picked up the baby and headed upstairs until I heard him leave the house.

* * *

Tears streamed down my face as that memory became too much to bear. Bent over in despair, with the water still running, I fell to the kitchen floor in grief. Nothing can explain the depth

MOVING ON | 61

The Beginning of the End

> *Nothing can explain the depth of pain I was experiencing at that moment.*

of pain I was experiencing at that moment. Perhaps nothing but my father's death, which would come four years later, even came close. Curled into the fetal position, I bawled. How would I go on? Fear, devastation and hurt were all I felt.

I had no idea how loud my wails of sorrow had been until I felt these tiny fingers moving up and down the middle of my back. My puffy eyes and swollen face looked up at this little person standing next to me, consoling me.

"Mommy, don't cry. We are going to be alright," Jay said.

What? I wondered in bewilderment. Was this really a 3-year-old little boy speaking words of comfort to me with the wisdom of an adult?

Jay's statement gave me strength like I had never experienced before. I believe God used that little boy, who I loved with all of my heart, to give me hope and the will to continue. In that moment I knew I had to get through this, because someone was depending on me; someone needed me far more desperately than my husband, who had walked out on both of us. If I didn't do it for myself, I would pull myself together for my son. No matter what happened, he deserved a parent he could trust not to abandon him physically, emotionally or mentally. I put the pity party on hold, got up from the floor, pulled myself together and cooked the best dinner ever.

I didn't think a child as young as him could understand

change like we were experiencing. Usually, the resilience of children lets them bounce back from most situations, but the truth is they do know and understand when something's wrong from the beginning. For years after my marriage ended, Jay feared being left alone. He didn't even like to be in a room by himself. If I left the room or stayed away too long he would soon start to look for me. He wouldn't want to admit it, but even today, more than 10 years later, I still see some remnants of this insecurity in his behavior. I realized that, as parents, what we do and say affects our children long after we have moved past a situation. My emotional breakdowns from that point on became even more discreet. I didn't want him to see Mommy upset all the time.

> *I realized that, as parents, what we do and say affects our children long after we have moved past a situation.*

While sitting at the table eating my dinner and watching my toddler pick through his, I dwelt on the scene before me. Dinner for two. As a young, strong, independent woman just a few short years ago, I had never allowed fear and failure to become my steady companions. I left the dishes on the table and reclined in front of the TV until I fell fast asleep.

I had to get my mind clear enough to think. There was work to be done. Finding a lawyer was first on the agenda. Problem was...I didn't know any lawyers. When James offered his lawyer, I thought he had lost his mind. He actually suggested we use the same attorney and make this an amicable split! That wasn't happening. Not by a long shot! Just how stupid did he think I was? It became obvious that he'd been planning this thing for months. For all I knew, he had the papers signed and in the mail. No, I would have to find my own lawyer and figure out where to begin.

The only one I knew at the time was my brother-in-law, and he didn't practice family law. I was clueless. So when a co-worker recommended someone she had used a few months earlier for a similar problem, I contacted him. Not feeling as though I had much of a choice, I scheduled an appointment, and 500 dollars later, I was in his office – bawling my eyes out while he checked his watch in anticipation of my leaving. Honestly, I think his demeanor was a shield to hide his apparent incompetence. His office was a mess, he never told me anything with certainty, and I got the impression he avoided a lot of my phone calls. I got nowhere with him and he got away with my 500 dollars.

The second lawyer was even worse! This time, the referral came from my hairdresser. Hairstylists must be psychologists in disguise. Women come in for their touch-ups and therapy sessions rolled into one. My hairdresser referred me to this big, abrasive Italian man, the oldest brother in a family law practice. He had dollar signs stamped across his forehead. His retainer fee was 1,200 dollars and he let me know up front that money was his priority. No money, no service. So again, between tears and sobbing, I sat down in his office and shared my story from the beginning. I was at the mercy of another stranger. He scribbled a few notes on a yellow legal pad and asked me some questions about James, like where he worked, what he did for a living and who his lawyer was. James' lawyer had a recognizable name because he had recently gotten some young kid with well-known parents out of a murder conviction, though the kid had just killed two people during a robbery a few months earlier. Just great! James had gone and gotten himself a local celebrity for a lawyer. I listened to my new lawyer talk about James' attorney, and then he asked me a few personal questions about my childhood, employment and family. Jotting some more notes on his legal pad, he politely escorted me back to the lobby to fill out a series of forms and documents. It was just as well, since I was getting lost in all of the legal jargon he was verbally dishing out.

His office looked more like a law firm compared to the first lawyer's, yet it had the same cold feel to it, only with more people. They moved about, walking past me as if I was invisible. Did they have any idea how hard it was for me to come up with this 1,200 dollars, not to mention what I was emotionally going through? I just wanted a facial expression of sympathy from someone. When I finished, I took the papers to the receptionist. She handed me a receipt, some documents indicating what information I needed to return to her and a payment schedule restating the hourly fee and when payments were due. I remember sitting in my parked car wondering how I was going to pay yet another lawyer money I didn't have to spend. Knowing I really didn't have a choice.

...how I was going to pay yet another lawyer money I didn't have to spend. Knowing I really didn't have a choice.

Over the next several months, he scheduled a few pre-hearing conferences with James and his attorney, and secured one or two

The Beginning of the End

intimidating preliminary court hearings, but always preceded the sessions by informing me of how far behind I was in the payments I owed him. This went on through the winter of 1996, until eventually he, too, was gone from the legal picture.

Over the course of a 19-month period I would eventually go through three attorneys. I couldn't keep up with the rent, bills, daycare, groceries and legal fees on my income. The $110 a week I sometimes received from James barely paid for the Montessori Daycare Jay attended. Falling behind on rent forced me to find a smaller apartment. Shut-off notices and threats of "disconnect" on my utility bills were a constant reminder of the struggle I had in front of me.

Life became nothing more than one battle after another. I struggled to get through each day's routine of work and being a mom. Mornings were hard, evenings were even harder. At night, as I leaned over the tub to run my son's bath, my tears helped to fill it. After putting him to bed, the quietness and loneliness became virtually unbearable. I'd lie there feeling like I couldn't go on. My mind lingered on the hopes and dreams of a future, family and the additional children I'd never have. My life would forever be changed, and stopping this change from happening was out of my control.

How had I gotten here? What went wrong? I felt like I was on a rollercoaster ride and so badly wanted to get off, but couldn't. Trying to get an understanding of what was going on

I was angry and sad, which made me feel scared and powerless.

was like running after a moving bus. I was emotionally distraught. I was angry and sad, which made me feel scared and powerless. As if I was being robbed with my hands tied behind my back while the robber took everything. Everyday I woke up gasping for air, feeling like life was literally being choked out of me. I tried desperately to find an escape from this nightmare that I just couldn't wake up from. Maybe if I could've dealt with one emotion at a time, it wouldn't have been so draining. But the feelings didn't come one at a time; they came all at once. Like a bulldozer.

Broken mentally, spiritually, and financially beyond repair, I struggled to keep up with what was happening. Handling so many responsibilities alone was really taking its toll on me. Facing my toddler at the end of the day demanded more attention than I had energy to give. While Jay was hugging my shins for support, I longed for someone to hold and comfort me, too. I felt so isolated.

Searching for some comfort, I began writing and this became my fresh air. I could breathe again when I put my thoughts on paper. In the morning, during work, at night, before bed – it was all I could do. Whenever I felt overwhelmed and needed a release, writing became a form of prayer. I would write down my thoughts because it was easier to express them that way. It was also important because I could keep track of my progress, the periods when I seemed to be doing better, as well as my emotional setbacks. There was no holding back from my journal, my new best friend. I would be brutally honest with myself and how I felt. It forced me to ask hard questions like: "What part did I have to play in all of this?"

Addressing those questions was a first step toward making

The Beginning of the End

peace with my situation. There really wasn't anything left to work out besides how I could move forward. Acknowledging where and how I had made myself vulnerable, as well as what I could've done differently, didn't make me feel foolish or weak. It served as the beginning of my strength and wisdom.

Seven

The Other Person

Think about it: *The biggest misconception of marriage is how it "feels." When couples share the same reason for marrying, it usually has a great deal to do with how they feel about the other person. "He makes me feel safe and secure." "She makes me feel strong and complete." "I feel all warm and fuzzy inside when I am around her/him." The problem is feelings change. Because of that, marriages based on feelings alone are doomed to eventually fail. If marriage is not based on how you feel towards another, what is it based on? Commitment.*

People just don't seem able to commit anymore. We're constantly changing. Not that all change is bad. Change can certainly lead to growth. But look at why you are changing and what you are changing from. Is it change you truly need – or are you running from commitment?

The days and months after our separation were undoubtedly the most difficult I had ever experienced. James continued this game of lies and manipulation, and he played it well. I made it easy for him because I was so naïve. He would call and say things like, "I just need some time. I need to get some clarity." This gave me hope that we would get back together. It caused a tug of war inside me; between my mind and my heart. My heart wanted to believe him, but my mind knew better. Having already started gaining the strength to move on, now I hesitated while hanging onto every one of his lying promises. I may have been naïve, but I wasn't stupid. James was certainly crazy. He was out of his mind if he thought he would get away with what came next.

"He what?" I asked in shock. "Absolutely not! I have the title, he doesn't."

When I answered the phone that day at work, I had no idea it would be a representative from my credit union. My family had been members nearly all my life, so the long-time employees knew me well. Stealing a car from me? James had gone too far. The voice on the other end identified herself as a credit union employee and then proceeded to ask me if I was aware that my husband had produced a copy of the title to our minivan with my signature, authorizing my removal of ownership.

"Well, Mrs. McKay, he brought a copy of the title in the other day. He explained that when you lost the original, you asked him to order another one without your name on it," she told me.

"That is not my signature. I have not signed a thing, and do not remove my name from any title," I said.

It struck her as odd that I hadn't come in myself, when he handed her the title and "my" signature, so she decided to call me. After she assured me that nothing had been done and she would wait to hear back from me, we hung up. A car? I wondered. Would he go through such deceptive measures to get a car? I grabbed my keys and headed to my supervisor's office. I made some excuse about having to leave for a family emergency. The half-mile drive from my job to James' took way too long. It turned out his mistress worked at the Secretary of State's office, and she helped him order a new copy of the title. How long had it taken them to plan this scheme?

This time I caught him by surprise. The last thing he expected was for me to come in armed with the information I knew about what he'd done.

"A car, James?" I asked, walking into his office. "Now you've stooped so low as to try and steal a car from me? I'm going to the police. Maybe they need to know about this little game you and your friends are trying to run on me."

The involvement of police always seemed to get his attention.

"No one tried to run a game on you, LaShon."

"Oh, really? What do you call ordering a new title and signing my name to it ?" I asked. "I'm sure the bank would like to know what one of its employees is doing: ordering illegal titles." One of his best friends lived in the Detroit area and worked for a major local bank branch. No doubt he had something to do with the "new" car title.

He tried emphatically to calm me down. Well you can just imagine the outcome. For once, he sat there looking dumbfounded. His little plan of stealing the minivan right out from under me blew up in his face. He lied, begged and pleaded with me not to go to the police and press charges. He even offered to come back home, hoping this would keep me quiet. I was planning to press charges anyway, until I got this weird visit at my job from some strange man claiming to be an investigator with some department for the state.

He just showed up out of the blue one day. I hadn't contacted anyone, especially an investigator. He had details of the incident and he was asking way too many personal questions. He was far too eager to find out what I wanted to do. I smelled "set-up" right away. This "investigator" was, no doubt, hired by James' lawyer. They would use everything I told him against me. Did they think I was wearing a "stupid" sign? I just let the whole thing go, partly because I didn't really want the van anyway and partly because my Dad said, "It's just a car." Due to the bank representatives' inquisitiveness, the van remained in both our names. The principle of the matter was my biggest issue. I could no longer see a glimpse of hope for us settling things in a cordial way. James had already demonstrated how little he thought of me. Stealing the van showed me how low he would go. He was willing to leave me with nothing!

And it didn't stop there. Dealing with him became just one deceptive, deceitful episode after another. He continued to call and come by for his weekend visits with Jay, as if nothing had ever happened. I actually think that in his mind, my reaction to the whole divorce should be to just go along with it, without any complaint or disagreement. He was ruining my life – and he didn't understand why I had a problem with it?

We have to get a divorce…we have to get a divorce…we have to get a divorce… The words would ring in my mind like a scratched "45" record on a 1970's turntable. Then I started thinking about the way he had phrased the statement. Don't people usually say they "want" a divorce? He said, "We have to get a divorce." What was up with that? I determined that I wasn't getting the whole story.

Something was missing.

*　*　*

I knew James was having an affair. How? Gut feeling. You can't rely on gut feelings? Says who? Gut feelings have helped solve many murder mysteries. Gut feelings have saved many lives. Sometimes you just know. A woman's intuition when it comes to her husband is powerful. Maybe men know, too, but a woman definitely does. Besides, James' behavior had never made sense in the first place. With a young, beautiful, smart wife at home, an adorable baby boy and plans to become a pastor, he had no reason to wake up one morning and announce that he was leaving his family. No one has to get a divorce. People choose to get divorced. They also do many irrational things when they find themselves involved in questionable relationships.

> *They also do many irrational things when they find themselves involved in questionable relationships.*

I had already accused James of having an affair. My first inclination that something wasn't right came from my 2 ½ year old in December 1995. Kids are so honest in what they say, and they have an impeccable memory. If we listened to children more, we could learn a lot. Driving home from church one sunny Sunday afternoon, I decided to take a different route. James and I often drove separately to church because of his responsibilities. Jay, strapped securely and contently in the backseat, was enthralled with the scenery outside his window. He kept his eyes glued to every passing image, determined not to miss a single detail. The sun was unusually bright. It was the perfect day for a leisurely drive, and we were in no rush to get home. As we drove down Nichols Street headed towards Main, Jay blurted out, "Mommy, I want to play with Christopher! I want to play with Christopher!"

Christopher? I didn't know of any little boys at his daycare named Christopher. What made him want a new playmate? Why would he suddenly want to play with a "Christopher?"

"I don't know of any little boys named Christopher, Jay," I answered.

"I want to play with Christopher," he said persistently.

His insistence caught me by surprise. Surely, he had gotten the name mixed up with another one. As I sat at a stop light, I searched my memory. We were always meeting people at functions, other churches, or in our neighborhood. But I couldn't recall a Christopher. Then it hit me that there was a little boy at the church, a good three or four years older than Jay. He would sometimes come to service with his mother and grandmother. As best I could recall, though, Jay had never played with him. I reserved play dates to kids more his age. Almost instantly, something moved in my spirit, and another Christopher came to mind. The light changed to green and I turned around to address my son, who was still demanding to see his new playmate, "Christopher."

"Jay, do you want to play with Christopher the girl or Christopher the boy?" I asked.

The driver behind me impatiently blew his horn, but I didn't move an inch until I got my son's answer.

"I want to play with Christopher the girl!"

My heart dropped into my stomach in astonishment.

As I rolled the car forward in slow motion, my mind went back to one of my first visits to Calvary Chapel Church. Late for the beginning of service, I slipped in and tried to quickly take a seat towards the back of the nearly empty sanctuary without being noticed. Belting out a note that I thought only Mariah Carey owned was a voice coming from the front of the sanctuary. With the choir swaying behind her in unison, she kept the congregation of about 50 people captivated with her commanding voice. Marlene Robinson was a middle-aged, single mother in our church, who looked vaguely familiar. But I couldn't recall where I'd seen her. She was a fair-skinned woman of medium height, with a "plain jane" look. Very unassuming. The features, if any, that stood out were her eyes. She had these big wide eyes that focused slightly past you to the right, as she looked at you.

The choir sang one more selection before she returned to her seat in the stands behind the altar.

"Amen, amen," the reverend said, approaching the pulpit, as he pulled everyone's attention away from the choir. I don't recall if James had invited me or if I had invited myself. Either way – big mistake. I was anxious to leave. Although I was raised Lutheran, a denomination that lacks a lot in the excitement arena of religion, this had to be the driest church service I'd ever been to. It felt cold and lifeless. A handful of elderly parishioners sat throughout the front of the church. They seemed to require the most assistance from the three or four ushers dressed in white uniforms, gloves and hats, and holding fans. The few young folk, obviously forced to come by their parents, were cramped into the last four pews in the rear. Their light whispers and giggles kept a few heads and stern, narrow gazes turned their way throughout service. The rest of the 50-or-so worshipers were middle-aged members, who I surmised had probably grown up in the church, politely nodding to the overly exuberant reverend hollering from the pulpit. I even saw James, who was sitting on the other side of the altar, jerk his head from a quick nod-off.

Fighting sleep and boredom, I sat there thinking to myself, "This can't be for real." It felt more like punishment than a time of praise and worship. Even the choir's songs reminded me more of a time of struggle than a time of joy and salvation. Resisting the urge to doze off, I let my eyes drift around the sanctuary, taking in the pale green walls that were badly in need of a fresh coat of paint. The dimly lit lights high above in the cathedral ceilings contributed to the dreariness throughout the sanctuary. I kept looking around until I landed on the 10 to 12 mostly women singers who made up the choir. When my eyes met Marlene's, they just stopped. She was looking at me, and it felt as if she had been for awhile.

Then, thank God, service was over! What resembled a wedding reception line was formed by old ladies waiting to greet and shake hands with the pastor.

"That was a mighty fine sermon you preached, pastor," they told him. Hadn't they done this every Sunday for as long as they could remember? Did they have to linger in that line for so long? When I finally reached the narthex and went to greet James and Rev. Chesterman, I didn't receive the reception or introduction I expected. Within earshot of others who had congregated in the area, he introduced me as a "friend." By that time we had been dating off and on for over a year. Certainly, I thought we were more than friends. That was it? Friends? The surprised and disappointed look on my face caused Rev. Chesterman to give me an even warmer welcome and handshake than I imagined he normally would. I politely whispered to James that I would wait for him outside. I forced a smile through the frown on my face as I passed the few people still standing around talking. I didn't quite know what to think about the way I had just been presented, but I would get to the bottom of it sooner than later. At the bottom of the four or five steps that led to the front door, I overheard Marlene introduce her daughter "Christopher" to someone else who was probably visiting for the day. That was the first time I became aware of the girl named Christopher. The girl my two and a half year old wanted to play with.

* * *

As I continued on the drive home with Jay, I searched my mind again. When had my son played with Marlene's daughter? Hard as I tried to recall ever taking him to visit this child, I knew that I hadn't. Like the other Christopher, she was at least four years older than Jay. But it was obvious that he had visited her enough times to recognize the street where she lived when we drove down it – which is the reason he had expressed his interest in playing with her.

"No, Jay," I finally answered. "Not today. We have to get home."

He seemed content with the answer and we drove the rest of

the way in silence. I, on the other hand, was uncertain about what to do with this newfound information. Even connecting it with whatever might be behind James' evasive behavior, I still tried to reject the signs.

My second indication came in the form of a confession from his best friend's wife Cam. It was another late night and I found myself waiting up again for James. This time I happened to call Bob, who he often hung out with at some bar or club downtown. Cam answered the phone. She and I were nothing alike. We would never have traveled in each other's circle if it weren't for our husbands. She was sweet, but different. Talented, but eccentric. Cam was a nurse at a major hospital in the city. In her spare time, however, she enjoyed dressing up as a clown and performing at kid parties. She'd even been the clown at Jay's first birthday celebration. Bob's and Cam's estranged young adult son was frequently getting in trouble with the law, and their teenaged daughter was also estranged. She went to an "alternative" school instead of regular high school. The closest Cam and I had been was right after Jay was born. When James brought me home from the hospital she was there with dinner cooked and beds made. She even stayed most of the night so I could bathe, eat and get used to managing my 3-day-old baby boy. As a new mom, I was grateful for her help.

"Hi Cam," I asked from my end of the telephone. "Is James over there?"

In her soft, whining voice, she said, "No, he isn't here."

"Oh, I thought he might be hanging out with Bob," I said, fishing for more information.

The Other Person

"Bob isn't here, either. He's out of town."

"Oh, I see."

"How are you?" Cam continued.

"Oh, I'm OK," I said, giving my usual quick response when I'm not OK. I think it was the tone of my voice that made her comfortable continuing with more questions. Over the next two hours she proceeded to fuel my greatest fear. She told me everything she knew, including details of James' weekend disappearance earlier that month. At first I didn't want to believe her. But I knew she wasn't lying. It was of no benefit at all to her to say what she did. She actually admitted that her and Bob had many arguments about his covering for James. She went on to tell me her own personal tale of betrayal by a cheating husband. Once again, young and naïve, I wondered to myself, "Is this some right of passage every married man must go through?"

> *I wondered to myself, "Is this some right of passage every married man must go through?"*

From my drive with Jay in the car a few months earlier, I had an idea where the "other woman" lived, but didn't know for sure. Cam gave me what she thought was her address. I lied when I assured her that I wouldn't do anything "crazy." Then I sat on the couch all night, waiting to confront James when he came home. He never did.

Needless to say, when I finally did confront him about Marlene, he denied it. The next night, he pulled the same thing. I decided I was going to catch him in the act. I called a sitter for Jay, told her I would be back in an hour, got in my car and headed to the address Cam had given me. It was well after 11 o'clock. I drove down the street to the house looking for our vehicle, but found no green mini-van. My windshield wipers were going pretty fast now. Raindrops on the window made it hard to see. I re-traced my path, but this time I went down the street a little farther. There it was. Our van – my van parked deep in the backyard of this little brick house so as not to be easily seen from the street. I froze. I saw what I was looking for, but fear gripped me when I saw it. What should I do? Knock on the door? Blow the horn? Then he'd come out. My portable car phone was in my purse at home, but it didn't matter. I didn't know her number anyway. At least 20 minutes went by while I sat trying to determine my next move. My greatest fear was realized. Sitting there in that cold, damp car I thought about how this would change our lives forever. Not until that moment did I know the feeling of betrayal.

Not until that moment did I know the feeling of betrayal.

I blew the horn loudly and long enough to wake up the entire city. I saw a curtain pull back in the top bedroom window, but no one came to the door. I blew and blew and blew until my sadness turned to anger. In a small fit of rage, I got out of the car, went to the door and rang the doorbell. No answer. I rang it again. Still no answer. I went back to the car and blew the horn again. I repeated the routine until I thought someone would call the police and they might haul me off to jail. But he wasn't getting off the hook that easily.

Later on, I found myself arguing with him. Demanding he be a man, come home and take care of his family. He pointedly told me he was taking care of his family. That Jay was his family and that didn't include me. Furious and hysterical, I headed back over to her house.

She answered the door as if she'd been expecting me. Her living room more resembled a laundry room. I didn't wait for her to invite me in. I spotted a place between a pile of folded towels and unfolded shirts, and sat down. Out of the corner of my eye I saw a big, bright-eyed little girl peaking around the corner. I wasn't there for long conversation; I was there to simply find out if this church-going choir member was sleeping with my husband.

"Marlene, I'm asking you first as a woman, secondly as a soror, but most importantly as a Christian: Are you sleeping with my husband?"

Her response caught me off guard.

"I don't make it a habit of sleeping with married men," she replied.

That was it. She said nothing else. I sat wondering what would make any woman pursue a married man. What, in all of Marlene's reasoning, allowed her to participate in an affair? She had a daughter, she went to church. She sang in the choir, for goodness sake! So what part of sleeping with a married man did she see as right. I wanted her to explain all these things, but for some reason I accepted her quick response of denial and left the house. That was in May 1996. My next encounter with her would be far more revealing.

***

There is so much shame that comes with discovering your spouse is having an affair. As I look back, I know it was shame coupled with fear and a sense of failure that kept me from reaching out to other people for support. I was the one who was embarrassed without a reason to be. I hadn't done anything wrong. Why was I feeling bad when it should have been my husband and the other woman who should have been ashamed?

This misplaced guilt is far too common in troubled marriages today and far too accepted as the norm in society. Even marriage itself is seen more as an arrangement than a life-time commitment. Have we done away with drawing the line and setting boundaries in our marriages? Have we forgotten to honor our vows? Is marriage more about emotional feelings that change from time to time, or is it about building a future with the person we love?

What's even scarier is how infidelity has surfaced in the church. Isn't the church supposed to be the one place where you can feel exempt and protected from the deceit and betrayal so common in the outside world? Isn't God's standard the standard to be recognized among people who call themselves believers? Apparently not, given the rise in the divorce rate among Christians. Certainly not in my case. When I needed my church the most, they not only turned their backs on me, they practically threw me out and nailed the door shut. My repeated calls to the denomination leaders were never answered. Not even the senior pastor or his wife made an attempt to speak with me. No calls, no contact. It was as if they had chosen sides before they even heard what I had to say. I was looking for something, anything from them. I needed them to express disapproval of what James was doing. Maybe even give him some formal reprimand. But it never happened. Shortly after they ignored me, I made the choice to leave. I couldn't stay at that church anymore. Instead of helping, it had become an environment that only interfered with my ability to heal. I couldn't allow anyone else's acceptance or compromise between right and wrong to cloud my own judgment.

> *I couldn't allow anyone else's acceptance or compromise between right and wrong to cloud my own judgment.*

When I finally reached out to my personal inner circle, I really didn't get the feeling that family and friends understood what I was going through. Their sympathy was appreciated, but not always helpful. Not having gone through a divorce before, they couldn't possibly comprehend my pain. It wasn't until my father died that I realized for the first time how true the statement, "You don't understand how I really feel" could be. You just don't know another person's suffering if you haven't personally experienced that same depth of loss.

People would tell me all the time, "You'll be OK. Everyday it will get easier and easier." My family seemed less patient. They wanted me to hurry up and get back to "normal." I wasn't my usual, upbeat self and they didn't like seeing me this way.

"Just snap out of it," my mother said one day after seeing me mope around the house. "How long are you going to mope around sulking after that man? He's moved on with his life, you need to do

The Other Person

> *You can't blink and have the pain disappear.*

the same. Obviously he's not thinking about you."

Her advice was easier said than done. I couldn't "just snap out of it." Who can turn their emotions on and off like a light switch? True, heartfelt love doesn't go away because your spouse walks out of your life. You can't blink and have the pain disappear. Did Mom think I liked feeling this way? Truthfully, I was sick of hearing the same old lines from family and friends. Who were they to tell me how I was going to feel? It wasn't their lives falling apart, it was mine.

The truth is that people handle divorce differently. There's really no right or wrong way to get through it because each circumstance is so uniquely different. We internalize hurt and pain in different ways. Our personalities allow us to mask the hurt in whatever ways we see as best. I stopped eating. Within weeks and months I had dropped four dress sizes. Sleep became a luxury that I experienced in spurts. Some people throw themselves into their work; I threw myself into my son. I hid behind my motherly responsibilities because that was the only place I felt like my life had value. And when I wanted to conceal my suffering, being the dotting mother was an easy way for me to pretend that I was okay. That everything was okay. I would prepare myself to leave the house, put on my best outfit, flawlessly apply my makeup, put every strand of hair in place and mentally psych myself up to face the world. I had it all wrong. I was trying to work from the outside in, instead of from the inside out. I wasn't being honest with myself. I needed to be honest with myself first, and then it would have come naturally for me to be honest with others. This meant finding strength in my moments of weakness. I didn't want to fold, but I wasn't sure how to push ahead.

This went on for nearly a year. While going through the motions of a normal life wearing a facade, on the inside I was a basket case. And as it turned out, I wasn't doing such a good job of hiding it anyway! Divorce affects every area and every relationship in your life. That's why divorce recovery is not just for those who have gone through a divorce, but for everyone who is impacted by it. The only person I was truly fooling was me. I put more pressure on LaShon than I put on anyone else.

I'm not even sure I knew the bad shape I was in. Normal responsibilities became everyday feats. Friends, family, co-workers and work itself were all way too much to deal with. This thing was overwhelming! I tried to keep the emotional stress restricted to just one location, like putting it in a jar. "I'll deal with it when I get home," I'd tell myself. At work, in the car or at the grocery store, I'd insist, "I'm not going to think about the divorce." But that was impossible and illogical. I was dealing with a powerful force of change. No matter how hard I tried, I kept coming up short on solutions for how I would handle it.

Because divorce has become so prevalent, I believe we all need to understand the recovery process. Even those who have not had the experience need to know how they can help those around them in their healing. During my workshops and counseling of couples,

I have heard both men and women say, "She got the friends," or "He got the friends" – as if friends were awarded as part of a court settlement. People who were once close to both husband and wife wonder who they should support after the breakup. In reality, both halves of a couple can suffer, even if their friends choose sides. Biased support doesn't always allow complete honesty. Going into our relationship, James and I pretty much had separate sets of friends anyway, so that wasn't much of a problem. The church members were the issue. It was amazing to me that the very people who should have had the capability to embrace us both didn't. The cold shoulder I often felt as the pastor's estranged wife intensified my sense of isolation even more. Though it soon became more than obvious what was going on between James and Marlene, I was still treated as if I had committed the sin. It said a lot as to where people's honor rests. Does what we teach others line up with what we believe?

When I tried to go to the one place where I should have received the most comfort, the most support – my church – I felt the equivalent of being left outside to shiver in the cold. They had wrapped their arms around their self-righteous assistant pastor and refused to see any wrongdoing on his part.

Then, just when I thought it couldn't get any harder, circumstances proved me wrong once again. Nothing could have prepared me for what came next.

Eight

Revelation(s)

THINK ABOUT IT: *Sometimes all we need is that one last sign. After the lingering tension, the suspicion, the arguments, the uncertainty and the hanging on to hope that our marriage will survive, the truth shines on our faces like a bright light. The question becomes, "Now what?" Once we recognize that final sign, do we prepare ourselves for what new adventures lie ahead in our lives, or do we ignore it and blind ourselves to the truth? Dangle too long from a thread of hope, in spite of all signs to the contrary, and like any thread, it breaks. The fall from a broken, worn-out thread can be a lot harder and more painful than knowing when it's time to walk away.*

As soon as she stood up, I heard it: "No! It's a lie! You're lying!"

This loud conversation taking place in my head made me feel dizzy. I sat down on the pew. I was certain everyone around me could hear the words, too. "This cannot be true! He would never do this to me. No, Lord…no…"

My face was buried in my hands. I gave her one more look as I lifted my head again. It was true. Marlene was pregnant. Oh no, Lord, please…this cannot be! I could endure anything. Everything. But not this. I couldn't take this. Right there in the middle of the song, in the middle of the afternoon service, it was revealed to me. How could I not have seen this before? I wasn't sure why my eyes didn't perceive it, but when the Holy Spirit drops something in your spirit, you hear it – like a ton of bricks falling! I no longer noticed the choir singing, the organ playing or the people standing around me. My mind had drifted to an unknown place. My body went limp like an overcooked noodle. I could only turn and look with disbelief at James. In that moment, his eyes caught mine and he knew I was aware of what everyone else in that church had known for months. He looked at me and his eyes spoke, seeming to say, "I wanted to tell you so many times, so long ago but couldn't." I dropped my head and concentrated my efforts on not allowing the tears that had welled up in my eyes to fall. There would be plenty of time for that later. After service, I gathered my things and left as quickly as I could without saying a word to a soul.

> *In that moment, his eyes caught mine and he knew I was aware of what everyone else in that church had known for months.*

I was expecting someone to come out any minute with a camera and announce, "You're on candid camera," putting an end to a cruel, humiliating practical joke. Unfortunately, there were no cameras because all of it was real.

As I arrived home, I thought, "Just make it to the bathroom. Make it to the bathroom." That's all I kept telling myself as I fumbled with the key to the back door. Fighting to keep down my morning's breakfast, I dropped my purse and the brochure from the afternoon program on the floor, stumbled over a few of Jay's toys in the living room and finally crouched down on the cold tile. Staring into the bottom of the toilet, I never felt so low. So hopeless and empty.

* * *

Mrs. Webber answered the phone as if she were expecting my call. Now I realized the reason for her visit six months earlier on that cold Sunday afternoon. She assured me that she'd be right over after we made arrangements for her daughter to take Jay to their house for a while. Not even a 3-year-old should be present for the kind of conversation that was about to take place between his parents. Mrs. Webber's daughter Angela had just completed her third year at Michigan State University. She had her mother's trained professionalism and her father's warm smile. I told her to bring Jay back before dinner in about an hour.

Neither of us said a word as I sat and James stood by the door. Not knowing what I was going to do or say, he probably thought that was his best position, next to the nearest exit. Literally, after about 10 minutes of silence between us, I started.

"James, we've been through so much together and what we are going through right now is undoubtedly the hardest thing I have ever experienced. I feel like I'm thinking the unthinkable here. What I'm about to ask you, I need you – really need you – to tell me the truth. No matter how much it will hurt me..."

"LaShon, I don't have time for this now," he interrupted. "You are obviously upset about something and I think you should go lie down, get some rest."

Avoidance. A common sign of guilt.

"Rest! Rest, James? I don't need rest. I need the truth from you."

"LaShon, this is not a good time."

"When is a good time, James? When will it ever be a good time for you to answer your wife this one question?"

He lowered his head and his tone changed. Now more helpless and defenseless he asked, "What, LaShon? What do you have to ask me?"

Even as the words were coming out of my mouth, I couldn't allow myself to think they were true. I couldn't believe I was even saying them.

"Is Marlene pregnant with your child?"

With a trained response, he looked me in the eye and told me, "No." Just like that. I wanted to believe him. I needed to believe him.

"James, I'm going to ask you again and I need you to tell me the truth. I need to hear from you – the truth.

"No, LaShon."

Truth is not hard to swallow. Lies are. As much as I would have given anything this side of earth to believe my husband on that day, I knew the Holy Spirit did not lie. He left my apartment. I lied down on my couch and listened to the silence in my apartment. I began to wonder if death would be better for me than this. What had I done to deserve such pain from someone I loved so much? Surely dying

If it weren't for my personal relationship with God, I know I wouldn't have made it.

had to be better than the cruel punishment I was being forced to endure. I nearly cried myself into a coma.

If it weren't for my personal relationship with God, I know I wouldn't have made it. Being able to draw on strength that only the Creator can give when all and everyone else fails is what got me through. How do you mend a broken heart? God is near to the broken-hearted. "I will never leave you or forsake you" were words of comfort and support I relied on. It didn't take away all the hurt, but I knew I wasn't alone when I prayed. There was a greater presence within, strengthening me.

I was no longer as sure of my feelings about James as I had been before. There was a drastic change in how I saw him from then on. It came mostly from his ability to, not once or twice, but continually lie to me without difficulty. His lack of concern for me, or what was being said throughout the church and the community meant nothing to him. Truth be told, he didn't seem to care for his child, either. My eyes were beginning to open. After all that time.

He stood by his denial and lie for two years before finally admitting the child was his. Thank God I didn't wait to hear the truth from him before I believed what my own inner voice told me.

Nine

"What God Has Joined Together, Let No Man Separate."

THINK ABOUT IT: *Every time you think of something that went wrong in your life replace that thought with something that went well. Choose to focus on the good. Life is just a sum of decisions we make on a daily, minute-by-minute basis. Dwelling on the bad choices we've made is a part of life we give way too much time and attention. Divorce doesn't have to be a bad situation. It's just an adjustment to something different. You can do a lot with "different."*

Marriage is hard work. I witnessed this firsthand with my parents, who'd been married for 38 years at the time of my fathers' death. I can recall witnessing many rough periods between them when I was a child. Looking at their struggles raising four children in inner-city Detroit during the 1970's and 80's should have been enough for me to know that building a family was a challenging experience. Somehow, some way they worked through it all. Our family's good times far outweighed the bad times. This is actually the case in a lot of our lives. Good outweighs bad. But during the rough periods, we tend to give the bad thoughts a lot more energy. I wanted the same joy of family living I had experienced as a child.

> The "rule" book on marriage needs to include details of the difficult times.

The problems of marriage, however, are too often ignored. We paint this perfect picture of what life will be like after marriage. When the wedding is over and the honeymoon ends many aren't prepared for the reality of married life. They want the sweet bliss from the courtship and it's gone. The "rule" book on marriage needs to include details of the difficult times. What to do when disagreements and disappointments occur, or careers collide. The biggest conflicts are not always about money or religion. Sometimes they're about basic things like time and attention. We have to stop entering marriage with blinders on.

* * *

Even after a rocky courtship, I never thought about a way out once I married James. It was 1992, and when I said, "Till death do us part" I was in it for the long haul. Excited about new roles as a wife and expecting mother, I prepared myself for a long life of working in the ministry with my husband. What God has joined together, let no man separate. Initially, I had a hard time with James' indifference to this. How dare he turn his back on the vows he made to me? Before God? Because I took them seriously, I assumed he did as well. But it's the condition of a person's heart that dictates his or her ability to honor vows. Overnight, the significance of our vows changed and I was left grasping for anything that would help me make sense of it all. When I finally went back to what I knew best and relied on the most for answers, direction and strength, I began to understand all these things. Reading God's word was becoming the medicine my soul ached to receive. Nevertheless, it was a long, gradual process before all the answers came and the pain subsided. Thankfully, the scriptures were still there to nourish me when the people who taught them were not.

James and I couldn't even get marriage counseling. I don't know if it was because the senior pastor Rev. Chesterman didn't know how to give it, or if it was because he was apprehensive about counseling a fellow pastor. I wondered how many marriages among leaders in the church ended because they had no counseling, or because they had inappropriate counseling. I often wondered – and still wonder – how many women endured an experience like mine. The secrets of infidelity and adultery among pastors and leaders in the church today are offensive to the point of being unspeakable.

> *The secrets of infidelity and adultery among pastors and leaders in the church today are offensive to the point of being unspeakable.*

At one point, the divorce made me feel as if I was letting God down. Like somehow I was a disappointment. I had failed in keeping my "till death do us part" promise. Did God hate me? Doesn't scripture say God hates divorce? Yes, God hates divorce, primarily because of the consequences He knows it will have on so many people involved; the lives that are going to be torn apart because of it.

Yet, He allows it. That's right: God allows for divorce. He has given everyone a free will. We are not puppets on a string, moving

> *Marriage is an act of two, but divorce is usually an act of one.*

according to His every pull. Of course, His hope is that we would choose the right way; that our actions will align with His word. But He is not a forceful God. So let's clarify the scriptures most commonly associated with divorce – God hates the practice, not the person.

It took months for me to understand that divorce doesn't always take two. Marriage is an act of two, but divorce is usually an act of one. I wasn't an equal participant in the decision to end my marriage. Divorce can occur because of a self-centered spirit. It is a selfish act, even though the decision can be a mutual one. Both individuals may decide they can no longer be married and end the relationship. But more often than not, it is the choice of one individual. It's deciding that the commitment once made to your spouse no longer has to be honored. You don't "have" to get a divorce. You choose to get a divorce.

I knew James was making this choice, and nothing I said or did was going to stop him. Whenever you find yourself in this position, there is nothing left to do but to let go, move on and find your place of peace. Show me a marriage that hasn't had its share of hard times and I won't believe you. The ability to stick it out and work through a situation speaks volumes about who you are as a person, about your character. During job interviews, potential employers take note of applicants who've changed jobs several times in the last few years. Why? They're looking for signs of dependability, loyalty and commitment. Do you have what it takes to stay committed?

Every marriage goes through difficulty, but only those marriages composed of individuals who understand and value commitment will endure the test of time and everything in between.

Ten

Stages of Recovery

THINK ABOUT IT: *Why is divorce so painful? Because it's an unnatural death.* Recovery from divorce is a process. Understanding how you feel and why you are experiencing complex, mixed up emotions all at the same time is a necessary part of recovering. The road can be a long, hard, difficult, one. Each stage in the recovery process is important and should not be ignored. How long you stay in one stage versus another depends on you. What is of most importance is that you continue through them. Each stage peels away and exposes a little more about ourselves than perhaps we want others to see, but each is vital and necessary for complete healing to take place. Don't let yourself get stuck in a stage and five or even ten years down the road find yourself dealing with the same issues in a brand new relationship.

The clouds were a foggy shade of gray. I opened the blinds anyway, hoping that the few streaks of sun behind the clouds would put a grin on my face and add a brighter outlook to the day. I'd been up for hours and was now on my second cup of lukewarm coffee. I moped around my already clean apartment wondering how I would fill the hours ahead: Jay was at his Dad's for the weekend and I had opted not to drive to Detroit. It would be another lonely

Stages of Recovery

> *I knew if I didn't get a handle on this, bitterness was soon going to turn to rage.*

weekend for me, partly because I felt uncomfortable around others and partly because I had a limited number of friends to call anyway. I filled my "to do" list with idle tasks just to keep busy. Most of the time, I didn't know if I was coming or going. At times, I still felt like an emotional basket case. Feelings came all at once and they came hard. If I wasn't crying I was angry. When anger passed I'd become depressed. Within minutes I could slip into a sadness, and only evil thoughts of revenge would bring me out of it. I knew if I didn't get a handle on this, bitterness was soon going to turn to rage. I was driving myself crazy!

But not really. Actually, I was going through the normal divorce recovery process, and I didn't realize it. What actually is divorce recovery? There is no one right way to make a transition after divorce. There are, however, common emotional experiences that people who have suffered loss go through. The stages of growth and recovery after divorce are similar to those we experience when the death of a loved one occurs. Long after my divorce, when my father died in 2000 I was able to recognize the stages of the grieving process I was experiencing. When you lose a loved one you need to grieve in order to heal. It's natural, normal and expected. We sympathize and empathize with others when they lose a loved one. If we understand that this grieving process must take place when someone dies, why don't we understand or allow ourselves to experience it when a marriage passes on?

Part of the healing process after the death of a loved one is the funeral or memorial service and burial. The funeral and burial bring a sense of closure for the loved ones left behind to mourn. What if there was no burial service after a death? What if every year, or month,

> *When a marriage ends in divorce...a death-like experience takes place.*

or week you had to re-enact the whole death experience for that person again? You couldn't do it. It would be impossible to move beyond that point in your life. When a marriage ends in divorce it is more than just the "dissolving of the marriage contract." A death-like experience takes place. Divorce recovery is the transition period and process one goes through during the end of a marriage and after a marriage ends. It is the healing process after the death of a marriage.

There are several stages of the recovery process. Not everyone experiences all of them in the same order, or in the same manner, yet each is significant.

~ Denial ~

"This could not be happening to us. I mean just a few years ago we were so happy," I heard one teacher say. "We were planning on buying our first home and bam! Out of the blue I was hit with divorce papers."

Another familiar set of lines goes: "Well I kind of knew it was coming. I mean it seems as though we had no other choice. We weren't getting along anymore. He was out all night...I wasn't inter-

Stages of Recovery

ested in him. We just stopped talking."

Both of these statements are typical of those who've experienced divorce. For some it comes as a total surprise, while others have been quietly anticipating the end. Regardless of how or why the divorce comes about, it still can be hard to accept – even when a person talks as if he or she is fine with this life-altering change. I've heard all types of stories. You can anticipate it happening, but somehow the reality is still a shocker. On the other hand, if you're not ready for it to happen and hoped it wouldn't, it's easy to just tell yourself that it's not taking place. You're in denial.

"He's going to come to his senses," you say. "She can't really be serious about this. I'll give her some space, time to cool off and surely she'll be back." Either you or someone you know is walking in denial right now because a mate has left the marriage. Going about things as if they're all business-as-usual won't change the circumstances. In fact, this approach will only make it harder to begin the healing process. Remember that denial is the refusal to accept reality. Actually, denial is the absence of reality. A friend of mine told me about one of his business clients, whose wife divorced him. It has been more than three years and the man refuses to let go. He hasn't changed a thing in the house. It's exactly the way she left it: the bedroom, kitchen, furniture. Everything. The man still believes she's coming back to him, and she is re-married!

Choosing not to believe the obvious doesn't change the obvious.

Choosing not to believe the obvious doesn't change the obvious. The reason we do this is to help dull the pain. Lingering in denial allows us to avoid fear. Fear of the unknown, the unfamiliar, fear of change. Fear of being alone. Fear of being around different people. Fear becomes this constant, unwanted companion. Maybe you've been married for five, ten, twenty years. Perhaps even half your life. For as long as you can remember your husband or your wife has been there. Every lasting mental recollection includes an image of him or her. Your new lasting memories won't. Perhaps you've never been alone and your biggest fear is loneliness itself. Or maybe it's a financial fear because you haven't worked in years and you have no idea how you will support yourself and your family without your spouse's income.

God has not given us a spirit of fear. The fear of what we will discover if we face the truth only keeps us living in the prison of denial. Not only has God not called us to live by fear, He tells us to have nothing to do with it. What makes denial so dangerous for spiritual people is that they often mistake it for faith. We say things like, "I'm going to stand on God's Word. I know if I pray hard enough, wait long enough, God will see to it that my spouse comes back home." This is very dangerous thinking. Maybe she'll come home and maybe she won't. There is always that hope and desire for reconciliation. If a marriage is restored, that is an ideal blessing from the Lord. However, ignoring the present condition is an unhealthy way of putting your life on hold.

> *Ignoring the present condition is an unhealthy way of putting your life on hold.*

Actually, denial contradicts faith because it doesn't acknowledge the problem faith is supposed to help us overcome. Refusing to believe what is happening right in front of us will not help turn the situation around. It keeps us hopelessly hoping. Believing there is no problem, or that the problem is not a serious one, only creates more problems.

Another reason for denial is that admitting failure in marriage, for many, means agreeing that there must be something "wrong" with them. Then there's what I call simplistic reasoning – insisting that a minor adjustment will repair the entire relationship. "If I change, then maybe he or she will come back. I'll change the way I look, cook something different, wear something different, get a different job." Reasoning that your change can bring about a change in the free will of another person is detrimental. If you've reasoned with yourself by using thoughts or statements like these, you are in denial.

Get real with yourself and answer some crucial questions like: Why won't I let go? What do I fear most? Do I want to hold on to this pain? Answering questions like these helps you come to grips with your reality.

Answering these questions truthfully was probably one of the hardest things I had to do. My difficulty in being honest was more toward myself than with others. Admitting my true feelings meant that I was vulnerable and not strong enough to get over this experience. I guess I figured that if I could convince myself everything was going to be OK others

> *My difficulty in being honest was more toward myself than with others.*

would believe it as well. I didn't want people to look at me and feel sorry for me. The problem, though, was that I couldn't hide from myself. No matter how many people I hid from, behind closed doors I still had to face me. It was extremely hard to admit that I didn't want to let go. I longed for and loved someone who didn't share the same feelings toward me. It became even harder to sort out the mixed emotions when feelings of love and hate collided.

If any of this sounds familiar, the first order of business is to determine what's kept you from moving on. Is it fear? Rejection? Embarrassment? Disappointment? Remember: You must be honest. If you start out lying to yourself you will lie throughout the whole process. Embracing the truth is your first step to emotional freedom. You don't like medicine but you take it anyway. Each step forward becomes a walk of faith.

Embracing the truth is your first step to emotional freedom.

One of the best definitions I've heard for faith is "trusting and believing God for anything and everything in our lives." Faith accepts that God will see us through the most difficult times and circumstances. He will provide the strength to endure whatever you must endure. Relying on Him gives you clarity, understanding and direction when you are faced with difficult situations and circumstances in your life. When you do this, you give God room to work in whichever way He deems best.

Stages of Recovery

~ Anger ~

I was so incredibly angry, and I had every right to be. But at what? At whom? There wasn't one simple answer to these questions. The object of my anger changed frequently. The slightest thing would set me off. Sometimes I was angry at myself for not being stronger and for giving in to the hurt and pain. The people in front of me in the grocery store line might even get the brunt of my anger for the day if they took too long at the checkout counter. But mostly I was angry at him. I was so incredibly angry at James! "How dare you do this to me? To your son?" was my constant thought. I was so angry because I had worked hard in a short period of time on a marriage that failed in spite of me. James ought to have been glad I married his sorry self. I'd show him. When this thing was all done and over with, he would be left high and dry. Anger fueled my insides like gasoline in a car. I was driven by thoughts of revenge. They gave me a rush of adrenaline that I used like a crutch to keep me going. I spent days and nights plotting how I could ruin my ex and make him pay. One time I came so close to slashing all four of his car tires that it felt almost like I was in a movie scene. Anyone who has ever been jilted in a relationship knows exactly what I'm talking about – that anger that seems like it can only be satisfied by watching your ex's suffering. Like brewing stew, my anger eventually turned to bitterness. The thought of James turned my stomach like the foul

There can be a place for anger in our lives that we can all use to push ourselves forward.

smell of rotten eggs. It ran so deep at times that I couldn't breathe. It was crazy! It wasn't all a waste, though. It kept the blood pumping through my veins when I wanted to give up. There can be a place for anger in our lives that we can all use to push ourselves forward.

Truth be told, usually when someone makes you that angry it's because your feelings of love for them run deep. People you don't have relationships with, or don't particularly care for, seldom get you going like those you love. We hurt most when we're hurt by the ones we care about. Anger can affect everything you do. It can change the way you view the simplest things and the way you respond to people. But don't let anger define who you are, even during difficult times. Like I did, you probably have the right to be angry, but who is it really holding back? Your ex is stealing something else from you by keeping you focused on anger: your control.

I found out that's what was really driving my anger. It was a sense that I had lost control of my life. I felt like he had the control and I had none. Want to even it out? Don't get bitter, get better. Focus on improving your life. Channel that energy into something that is going to make you feel more accomplished. See your divorce for the positive opportunity it can bring, not for the negative. You have a chance to start over. Isn't God a God of second chances? Take this second chance opportunity and run with it. You have more control of what's happening than you think. Control your choices. Will you choose to be angry, bitter, vengeful? And for how long? A month,

You have more control of what's happening than you think. Control your choices.

six months or even a year? Focus on what you can control directly – how you choose to view the present day, tomorrow and the life you have in store for the future.

~ Depression ~

It seems like every time I turn on the TV there's a new advertisement for some medical breakthrough drug out there to help fight depression and every other ailment plaguing us. The amount of medicine on the market is enormous. You're likely to get depressed just trying to decide which one to take! Thank God this wasn't the case ten years ago, or at least the "remedies" weren't advertised so heavily. There were, however, things like alcohol, overeating, undereating, casual sex, bad relationships or illegal drugs to turn to for comfort. Many of us do turn to one of these forms of "medication" when no other source of help seems available to relieve the pain. If you're fortunate enough to avoid the aforementioned self-destructive habits, you may still not be so fortunate when it comes to the poor self-image that can result from ending a marriage. Believe it or not, this can be more mentally and emotionally destructive. I stayed clear of all the chemically addictive vices like drugs and alcohol, and I avoided casual sex. But the emotional stress I took on caused me to lose a great deal of weight without trying to. Of course, this wasn't good for me, and it took me a while to shed the stress and get back to my normal, healthy physical shape.

Realizing that life as you've known it has been shattered into a thousand pieces like a puzzle that can't be put back together forces you to re-group, but you have no clue how you're supposed to pick up all those pieces and continue. These feelings are the root of depression.

But the problem isn't with feeling depressed. It's staying depressed. When is enough really enough? At what point do you close the door on your past?

But the problem isn't with feeling depressed. It's staying depressed.

For me that point was April of 1997. James and I had been separated for nearly a year with no movement towards reconciliation. The divorce was being prolonged through the bureaucracy of the court system. I was struggling and tired of the whole situation. After all, I was a strong person who knew early on that God had something special for me to do with my life. And I was 100 percent sure that how I was feeling wasn't going to help me achieve it.

The only comfort I had developed became the thing I grabbed and held onto for dear life: I saturated my mind with scripture. It helped get me through each day. The words, "I would have despaired unless I had believed that I would see the goodness of the Lord in the land of the living. Wait for the Lord, Be strong..." gave me the strength to make it through each day. No, it wasn't always that simple. Reading a few scriptures didn't instantly make me feel better and cure my frustration, but it gave me peace and contentment which helped me to persevere.

I began taking this scriptural "medicine" more often throughout the day. In the quiet of the morning before my toddler awoke, during break time at work, while I ate lunch at noon and always after dinner

> *I can't tell you how much reading the word reminded me of God's love, His plans to prosper me and His promise to take care of me.*

right before putting Jay down for bed. I found myself reading, studying more and more. I can't tell you how much reading the word reminded me of God's love, His plans to prosper me and His promise to take care of me. God wanted to give me a future and hope – to relieve the pain that was applying so much pressure on my heart.

What I read began to change the way I was thinking about my experience and about life itself.

~ Loneliness ~

The other day I was reading a newspaper article that stated: "Americans try to connect in a society where isolation is increasingly common." I thought, "Now how could that be?" Between the cell phone, e-mail, "instant messaging" and "text messages," how in the world could loneliness be so prevalent in our world today? The numbers are staggering. America's population is close to reaching the 300 million mark, we have greater means of reaching people than ever before imaginable, yet and still an authoritative study in the American Sociological Review found that the average American has only two close confidants with whom he or she can confide about important matters. Loneliness has become a lifestyle all its own.

While the article went on to discuss the excruciatingly painful feelings of isolation among middle-aged singles, "empty nesters" and the elderly, it failed to include in its group study another significant cluster of people – the once, but no longer, married.

No one likes coming home to an empty house after living with a spouse and family. It was funny how quickly I'd gotten used to having James around after such a short marriage. I'm sure being raised in a large family where someone besides me was always there didn't help the situation much. I dreaded the weekends when Jay would be with his Dad. I struggled to find new ways to occupy my time, but I had isolated myself from most potential company. I wanted to avoid the questions, the long stares and the patronizing comments people seemed to offer without invitation. Much of my isolation was self-imposed. Pain can cause you to create walls around yourself that are so thick no one else can get in; nor can you get out.

> *Pain can cause you to create walls around yourself that are so thick no one else can get in; nor can you get out.*

All of the various recovery stages can begin to feed off of each other. If you're not mindful of how to respond at each stage, you may find yourself in a vicious emotional cycle, creating a hole inside you that eats away at your life. How does this happen? The next relationship, if you dare to enter one, becomes a reflection to you of everything that went wrong in your marriage. You've started a relationship before you were ready, just to get over the loneliness. Your new significant other doesn't have a fighting chance. And neither do you.

Stages of Recovery

The recovery process is not easy, but it's essential. It calls for you to search your inner world and be truly prepared to address what you find there. Acknowledge that you and you alone are responsible for your healing.

> *I began to embrace my alone time and not fear it. I learned to separate loneliness from being alone.*

I didn't want to take responsibility for a problem I didn't create. But I had to. The choices were to either stay glued to this hurt, or allow it to teach me something new about myself. As long as I was glued to choice number one, loneliness was a forgone conclusion.

But you are never truly alone. "I will never leave you or forsake you" is a scripture I have highlighted in my bible. What strength it gave me during that first year when I felt all by myself! To know that, even if I couldn't see or touch Him, God was helping me sort through all the confusion made a difference in my recovery.

I began to embrace my alone time and not fear it. I learned to separate loneliness from being alone. When I felt lonely, I admitted it and forced myself to be around others, call a friend, go to a movie or to the store. I wouldn't let loneliness win. I wouldn't let it grip my heart or paralyze my body and mind. I fought back! Then during those times when I was content being alone I felt a sense of peace. I would focus on me and spend that time doing things that made me feel good about myself. I focused on acceptance. The quietness became more comforting. I didn't run so fast from my inner thoughts. Instead, I gave myself a chance to get to know and understand them.

By the same token, there are times when we can be so eager to avoid loneliness that we fail to protect our private space. I remember a day after my divorce was finalized when I went to get Jay from his daycare. The parking lot was full after another long, tedious work day. I appreciated the quiet time I spent while waiting in the car for a space to become available as the other vehicles departed. This was nothing unusual around 5 p.m. weekdays; it was always busy at the Montessori Day Care. For the most part, I liked the daycare. The teacher-to-child ratio was low, there was a good blend of boys and girls and it was very diverse. I was also quite impressed with the Montessori style of teaching.

I closed my eyes for a quick minute as I exhaled and thought about Jay's first day at the center. James and I had taken him there together. I definitely had a harder time with his first day than Jay did; this type of separation was brand new. After nearly two years of unsuccessful child care situations – trying to find someone dependable to provide in-home babysitting, or another decent home-based program – I was ready to place Jay in a stable environment. That first day, he immediately went in and started playing with a few toddlers. While conversing with the director, James and I watched our sociable son make new friends.

As I reflected, someone tapped on my window to say hello and motion for me to pull into the parking space next to hers. I smiled and moved the car in the direction of Nancy's gesture. She was nice. I didn't really know her, but we always struck up conversation with each other as we seemed to pick up our kids at the same time.

Plus, Jay and Morgan, her daughter had hit it off as friends from the beginning.

"Hi Nancy, how are you?" I asked, adjusting my sunglasses in the bright April sun.

"We got the invitation for next Saturday," she answered. "I can't believe Jay is almost three," she said.

"I know," I answered. "They're just growing up too fast..."

Waving goodbye to Nancy, I nearly ran over another parent as I rushed inside.

"Oh, excuse me!" I exclaimed. "I'm not watching where I'm going."

No problem. I'm Lizzy." Hi, I'm LaShon, Jay's mom. Jay was no where near ready to go. I could see him out the window still engrossed in his mountain climbing game of tag on the hill out back, with about four other little boys. After speaking to Miss Tate, his teacher, Lizzy and I walked out back to retrieve our kids.

Ana, her little girl was a year older than Jay and had only started attending the daycare about two months earlier. Because James and I had begun alternating Jay's pick-up days I hadn't noticed any newcomers to the center.

"I've only seen your husband...um...I mean Jay's Dad," Lizzy remarked. "He always picks him up."

"Yes, Jay's Dad and I alternate," I said, clarifying her previous statement and nudging Jay towards the door as I added, "It was nice meeting you."

"Mommy, can Ana come to my birthday party?" Jay abruptly blurted.

Suddenly caught with two pairs of hopeful eyes on me – Jay's and Ana's – I had no other choice.

"Sure, if it's alright with her mother." As if anticipating my response, Lizzy quickly said yes. I had the feeling that somehow she had already known about the party. We exchanged phone numbers and I gave her our address in the parking lot.

Before I knew it, Lizzy had become a close acquaintance. At her insistence, we shopped together, took the kids to "story time" at Barnes & Noble bookstore, and we even hung out together during weekends when Jay was with his Dad. Sometimes her friendship felt intrusive. She was inquisitive. Always full of questions. But I chalked it up to her personality. Then later, my feelings about her intrusive ways proved to be founded. One afternoon, unannounced, I went to the center to take Jay a change of clothes. It had rained off and on most of the day, but I knew that wouldn't have stopped a bunch of toddlers from playing in rain puddles that turned to mud. As I arrived with the clothes, Lizzy and James were startled to look up from what appeared to be a deep conversation and see me standing in the doorway. When I had introduced them at the birthday party, they acted as if they were meeting for the first time.

From that point on, I made it a point to limit my interaction with Lizzy. She had latched onto me for more than just friendship – she latched onto me for the purpose of gaining some kind of information. I never proved her communication with James was any more than harmless chat, but the evidence isn't what mattered: What mattered is that I felt uncomfortable about her intentions. Lizzy became a member of my outer circle. I couldn't take any

> *Choose your company the way you'd choose expensive jewelry – very carefully!*

chances dealing with people who may not be positive additions to my support system, and neither can you. Build your inner circle with positive, productive people. Don't ever let loneliness make you so vulnerable that you forget to take your time getting to know people. Choose your company the way you'd choose expensive jewelry – very carefully!

~ Acceptance ~

Just when you think it's over, wham! You're hit with another emotional blow. You've gone two or three whole days without shedding a tear. Then all it takes is a sentimental thought or that song that comes on the radio, and you're drifting back down memory lane. You begin wondering if it's ever going to end.

Acceptance was, by far, the hardest stage of the recovery process for me. Allowing myself to accept the divorce, meant giving up. No amount of praying or crying out to God for Him to cause a change of heart in my husband was going to make a difference. It meant that I would have to close the door and end the chapter to that part of my life.

I made my final attempt to reconcile with James around the spring of 1997. My doctor had ordered me off work while he treated a severe case of tendonitis in my right forearm, wrist and hand. The sharp, shooting pains were a physical indication of the amount of stress I was under, but the timing of this leave of absence couldn't have been more heaven-sent. Somehow I knew the next six weeks would mean more than just sitting at home and nursing an aching wrist. It meant healing the last remaining wounds of a broken heart.

It had been close to a year since Jay and I moved into the new apartment. There had been so much going on that I felt like I had to schedule time just to think. The divorce proceedings had dragged into their thirteenth month. I was exhausted in every sense of the word, but it was time for me to take some action. It was a bright, sunny Saturday morning and there wasn't a cloud in the sky. James' mom was planning a visit for Jay's fourth birthday in a few weeks, and my parents wouldn't have a problem driving up from Detroit. It would be the perfect opportunity for us to sit down as a family. If James wouldn't come clean with me, maybe he would feel pressured to do so with our parents.

After cake, ice cream and a non-stop hour of taking pictures of Jay riding his new bike, he settled down in his room to play with the tons of other toys he was given. I remember thinking that some of his gifts would have easily covered both my light and gas bills, which were scheduled for shut-off any day. As I walked back into the living room, the family was engaged in small talk, obviously waiting for the initiator of this little post-celebration meeting to lead the conversation. I really didn't know where to begin. Honestly, I wanted everyone to just yell at James, "What the hell are you doing?" If everyone would attack him with guilt, questions about his moral character – maybe even a little light violence – I thought he would somehow come to his senses again. But that didn't happen.

Of course, I started with the lingering question, "Why do we have to get a divorce?" Then, for the next hour and a half, James stuck to his guns, continuing to defend his position. None of our parents could sway him or make sense of his ridiculous lies and explanations. Sitting there listening to him talk really was something. No one likes the feeling of being rejected, and until that moment, rejection was all I had felt. As I sat there quietly and calmly listening to his pathetic words conjuring up one lie after another, I made a decision — I no longer wanted him. As if a light bulb went off in my head, I realized he wasn't ever worthy of me. That was empowering! I was in control again once I let myself clearly see how little of our former relationship still warranted a struggle. Acceptance was the first stage at which I recognized my choices. Reality set in and denial was a thing of the past. In that moment I learned a simple truth that my aunt would tell me sometime later: "You don't want anybody who doesn't want you." James had made his choice. And now I had made mine. It was time to end thoughts of saving the marriage. For good.

> *Acceptance was the first stage at which I recognized my choices.*

A change took place in me. Up until that point, I had reacted to everything that was happening. Now it was time for me to make things happen. I had finally moved through denial, fear, depression and even anger. My acceptance had arrived and was here to stay.

Within eight weeks my son and I moved. I was on the road,

emotionally, mentally and physically, to recovery. I was fortunate enough to have my job transferred and a loving family waiting to support me in the transition.

* * *

Though I realize this is not plausible for everyone experiencing divorce, consider changing your environment, if possible. A new outlook and a greater sense of acceptance can be aided by a change of location. One reason we resist letting go of attachments to the past is to avoid the feeling that we've lost. Sports fans understand. When the game is down to the last thirty seconds, the score is so close and one more outstanding shot or a miraculous play could change everything – but then the buzzer sounds – it's an unbelievable feeling of failure. They sit there on the bench, wishing for one more minute, or even a few more seconds, to try and change the result of the game. Dragging themselves off that bench and taking the long walk to the locker room is their final acceptance of defeat.

But it's a trap of the mind if you lose your will to let go of the past. Every month, every day, every minute, every second of your life now depends on your ability to let go. Holding onto the past doesn't allow you to grab hold of the future. On the other hand, letting go of a challenging marriage isn't the same as letting go after you're already divorced. If you are still married, seek counseling. Do everything feasible to save it. But know how to recognize when you've done all you can. Divorce recovery requires that you stop mentally tormenting yourself.

I used to wear my "victim" mask around friends and family to remind them of how badly I had been wounded, but around other associates and church members I didn't want to appear bruised. It was another form of mental torment for me to be more concerned about how others saw me than how I could get over the feeling that every valuable hope, dream and memory had been stolen from me. Being victimized by a stranger was one thing, but being victimized by someone I loved was far worse. I had to change my thinking.

> *Being victimized by a stranger was one thing, but being victimized by someone I loved was far worse.*

I once heard a pastor say: "Renewing the mind is evident by change. If you win it in the mind...you will win it in life. If you lose it in the mind, you will lose it in life." I experienced another light-bulb-in-the-head moment!

If I didn't get a grip, I might not ever get back on track. There is an aura that radiates from us when we feel good about ourselves. It commands respect from others. However, if we de-value ourselves, they will too. How can they do anything else? They have no other example to follow. We must know that we are worthy and deserving of love. We have to own our thoughts and own our happiness. You alone are responsible for your healing. There is so much more power in our thinking than most of us even know. It can change our reality. The Living Bible states: "Don't copy the behavior and customs of this world, but be a new and different person with a fresh newness in all you do and think. Then you will learn from your own experience how His ways will really satisfy you."

While I used to look at life through mirrors of what I didn't have and allow that to dictate what I did, now I look at what I want, and I focus my energy on getting it. I had a hard time trusting anyone. Yet, I still had an inward desire to be free from all the baggage I'd carried around for two years. I was sick and tired of being sick and tired, and I wanted to be happy

I was sick and tired of being sick and tired, and I wanted to be happy again.

again. I wanted to start over, so I wasn't going to quit until I found a way.

~ Forgiveness ~

It was once my goal to cause James as much pain as he caused me. I would recount the events over and over again in my mind. They gnawed away at me like an enormously bad toothache whenever I saw or thought of him. The anger was my defense and I held on to it tighter than a drowning man in a deep swimming pool holding on to a flotation device. After all, he was responsible for the way I was feeling. Wasn't he? The notion of forgiving him was inconceivable. He was going to "pay" for what he'd done. The longer I held on to these feelings, the more he was going to suffer. Forgiveness was a life preserver that had been thrown to me, but I refused to let it pull me to safety. Instead, I wrapped bitterness around me like a security blanket. I took it everywhere. I couldn't embrace any new experiences. I couldn't do anything that resembled forgiveness. I was bound by the anger.

But if misery loved company, why did I feel so isolated? We didn't talk much, but when we did James sounded as if he didn't have a care in the world. Something was wrong with this picture. He was supposed to be suffering because I had refused to forgive him! But I was the one who was filled with so much tension that, at times, I'd become physically sick. I had to get this poison out of me.

What is forgiveness? Is it acting as if the events that hurt us never happened? Is it walking away from them and not dealing with the reality of their consequences? Is it letting the person who offends us off the hook (whatever that means)? Does the offender have to be present in order for the offended to exercise forgiveness? Who and when should we forgive?

I didn't like the thought or the feeling of this whole forgiveness notion. It seemed way too easy for him and it seemed that, once again, I was getting the short end of the stick. Every time Jay asked, "When is Daddy coming home?" I was painfully reminded of when James walked out. Even now at the age of 13, when anger and resentment begin to surface in Jay's eyes, I have to choose my words wisely, so as not to perpetuate the same hostility. I have to help him work through his own pain which is a different type of pain than mine. He sees what I do to provide for him and he recognizes some of the ways that having his father's support would make things easier. How can I forget the past with my son's pain is right there in my face? Part of my anger was for what my son had to go through. In a divorce situation where children are involved, forgiving can be especially hard. But forgiveness doesn't necessarily mean that you forget. It does, however, mean that you pardon, or release, the offender. First for yourself, then for him or her, and others. Contrary to what you may think, the act of forgiveness mainly benefits you. When you forgive the person who has offended you, you release the anger, bitterness, and pain associated with the offense. You are the one who receives the reward of deliverance. Think about it: Whoever you are holding a grudge against has, no doubt, moved on – or you'd probably have less reason to hold a grudge! If that person spent time trying to apologize to you and correct things, you probably wouldn't have such resentment. But usually, the people who offend you are living without any thoughts of the anger you have towards them.

Contrary to what you may think, the act of forgiveness mainly benefits you.

I was stuck in revenge mode, even though I knew God said, "Vengeance is mine; I will repay." That wasn't enough. My plan was to help God out! I had to see James' pain and suffering. In reality, I was wasting away from so much anguish and bitterness that I was dying inside. I was wasting valuable energy on someone who was no longer that important in the whole scheme of things. Forgiveness started in me. It always starts with an offended person's ability to let go of the desire to punish or harm the offender. It's a choice to let go of resentment towards the person or persons who've hurt you. No doubt, this takes a true act of self-will.

If you ever find yourself stuck in a state of denial, or slipping back into the mindset of depression and bitterness, try this exercise to help rid yourself of the strongholds that have you stuck. Instead of letting thoughts and worries about your situation consume an entire day the way they used to consume mine, give yourself a 15- to 30-minute interval to focus on sadness, anger, disappointment or whatever emotion you need to express. Then take the rest of the day off from dwelling on the problem by reminding yourself that time is up. It's best not to start your days or end your nights with these 15 to 30 minutes, because it will be hard enough, at first, just to maintain a positive focus. You don't want to enter a new day with draining thoughts, or carry them with you to sleep. When I used the 15 to 30 minute exercise, it helped me categorize my priorities, and after practicing for some time I didn't need those intervals anymore. I had kept my negative energy and thoughts restricted to a time frame, rather than letting them spill over into my every waking thought. This is important: allowing yourself time to feel, while properly processing each feeling. Keep that in mind and recovery will be a natural result of your effort.

Who and what do you need to eliminate from your life? I don't mean by doing anything violent or drastic. I mean to whom, or to what, should you add physical, mental and emotional distance? This is an important question. In starting over, you are going to have to remove certain familiar people, places and things from your path. Why? Because your associations need to be purpose-driven. For example, maybe there's a mutual

In starting over, you are going to have to remove certian familiar people, places and things from your path.

acquaintance who likes to gossip and tell you things about your ex-mate: "She's dating so-and-so now...," "He bought a new car...," "I see her every time I go to the hairdresser..."

Why should you care when you're busy trying to live your life to the fullest? These acquaintances don't always mean any harm; in fact, sometimes they actually think they're doing you a favor by reporting on your former spouse's every move. But you don't need those types of distractions. If you reach a point with your ex when you can become good friends it can be a blessing – after all, a friend is always better than an enemy – but until then, don't concern yourself with her or him. It may become necessary to change those lunch dates with that gossiping mutual friend to occasional telephone calls. You don't have to be mean about it, but by directing your energies and attention in more meaningful directions, you'll honestly be able to say that you don't have the time for a lot of conversation. Of course, if the acquaintance really cares about you, you should be able to simply say you don't care to know what's going on with your ex and have the request honored.

Or suppose there's a place of leisure, like a restaurant or health club, that you regularly visited while you were married. The last thing you may want to see when you're at the gym to work off stress is your ex on the treadmill next to yours! Does this mean you have to give up your favorite places and change your routine? Not necessarily, but depending on how far along you've progressed in your recovery it might be a good idea to choose a new hangout, or, at least, a new time to visit. Remember, I even changed my church environment when it was no longer healthy or comforting to me.

Stages of Recovery

> *You don't want to let any of your past associations distract you from your goal of a life filled with peace and joy.*

You don't want to let any of your past associations distract you from your goal of a life filled with peace and joy. It's worth the sacrifice to drive a few extra miles to a new grocery store or choose a new place to have business meetings, if it helps you avoid slipping back into bitterness and resentment.

A wise saying goes: "A soldier standing alone is an easy target for the enemy." I don't know who said it, but it's true. Everybody needs somebody to lean on during difficult times. That's human nature. I spent a lot of time by myself unnecessarily because I wouldn't reach out for support. We push people away because our ability to trust has been bruised. But when we make everyone else pay for it, we wind up paying the most. Your responsibility is letting friends, family, co-workers, church members and anyone else you know that you can trust; know how they can support you. If you need a form of help they can't provide, seek out a divorce recovery group, personal counseling, telephone hotline, on-line resources, or a seminar on recovery. Because of the growing number of divorces in the church today, some have stepped up to provide forms of assistance to their members. The bottom line is you can't give up. Your survival depends on it.

Eleven

Making the Move

THINK ABOUT IT: *An eagle is meant to soar high above the altitude of any other bird. He never seems to tire, but gains new strength the higher he flies. Letting go of the weight that comes with needing to blame someone else for your situation will allow you to rise high like an eagle. Once you've truly let go, you'll release your ex-spouse, the "other" man or woman, your ex's new mate and everyone else from any ties, obligations or responsibilities to your own mental and emotional stability. It can be extremely challenging because you won't have anywhere else to lay the "blame." But the higher you fly, the more stamina you'll gain for continuing on your journey to full recovery.*

While thumbing through the Yellow Pages in a bit of a final attempt to secure a lawyer before my Monday morning hearing, her name leaped off the page: "Attorney-at-Law B.J. Weiner." She was located downtown on North Rose Street. My last two lawyers had been men. If nothing else, a woman would be a welcome change.

Right there in my cubicle at work, I dialed the number.

"B.J. Weiner speaking."

"She answers her own phone?" I thought to myself. I was expecting a secretary or, at the very least, a paralegal.

"Yes, hello. I am calling to get some information. Legal information."

"How can I help you?" she asked.

Surprised by my own comfort level, I started giving her details of my story from the beginning and went straight through to the end. I didn't come up for breath until she knew everything. I was certain not to leave out a single detail, not even about the two previous jerks I had for lawyers. James was trying to get full custody of Jay in order to keep me from moving a two-hour drive away, and I was due in court in three business days. At one point I started sobbing right there at work. All B.J. did was listen. She never interrupted. Even between sniffles, she listened until I was finished.

"I will be in court all morning, but you can come in tomorrow at 1," she finally said.

And that was it. I thanked her, more for listening than for the appointment, and told her, "I'll see you tomorrow."

That calmed my ever-failing nerves for the moment and gave me some hope that all was not lost. At least now I had a fighting chance. It was happening and I knew it. More changes were soon to come, but it was time to push ahead. If I was going to get my life back on track, I needed a fresh start. I needed to be around people who loved me and cared about my happiness. Even while I hesitated, I knew where God was leading me. Back home to Detroit.

It would be a long, grueling six months of documents, court hearings and still more emotional upheaval before I could say it was over. Then, almost to the day of our wedding, we signed divorce papers...five years later.

I felt strangely different. As though an important part of my life was coming to an end. That's because it was. But what I had to remember was everything in my marriage wasn't bad. One of the greatest joys of my life came out of it, my son. Some other things came out of it as well: growth, strength, new lessons in life, deeper love of myself and a deeper love and understanding of God. Could I have learned these things without a divorce? Perhaps. But the important thing is I learned them in spite of the divorce.

But the important thing is I learned them in spite of the divorce.

I believe life is nothing more than a book for which all of us write pages and chapters every day. I was ending one chapter in my book of life and beginning another. The awesome thing about this was that I had the power to direct how the next chapter would be written. We can't always dictate the outcome – how our chapters will end. But each day contains the power to decide how a new page will read. We can write pages and chapters filled with interesting facts, exciting adventures, creative quotes, funny pictures. Or we can write one sad, boring page after another.

Closing out the chapter that contained my divorce gave me the opportunity to move on to the next one. To create something new and see what else was inside of me, desperately needing to come out. What happened? I discovered more there than I'd ever imaged. I moved from victim to victor. Realizing that we're not victims causes us to walk with our heads held high. We stop being spectators in the game of life and become competitors.

Making the Move

Nothing but God carried me through it all. I recalled as a child hearing the chorus of a familiar church song, "He makes a way out of no way." Now it's more than a Sunday morning hymn. That song became reality for me. God literally made a way out of absolutely no way for me.

* * *

So what is the correct response when your spouse decides he or she wants a divorce? Do you fuss? Fight? Get angry? There is no general answer or response. Reactions will be as varied as the individuals reacting. Whatever the outcome, you have to see divorce as one small thing that has happens in your life, not your life in its entirety. Don't give it more power than it deserves. Who you are and who you are meant to be did not start and stop with your marriage or divorce. Go through this challenging time with dignity. Have respect for yourself and everyone else involved. There will come a point when you look back on this period and won't want to be haunted by memories of the behavior you displayed. Time really does heal wounds.

The more I grew, the more I wanted to keep growing.

I finally knew I was on the right track when I didn't find myself locked in my apartment all weekend thinking of the past. When my days started without their first thoughts being about my ex-husband I knew I was making progress. I could smell flowers again, laugh with friends or watch a movie alone without needing company. The more I grew, the more I wanted to keep growing.

130 | MOVING ON

* * *

So what have you always wanted to do? If you could do anything you wanted, what would it be? Maybe this is the time for you to try it. Make a list of five things you would do if you had no limits. Would you take a trip to Africa? China? Asia? Would you open that quaint, French-style coffee shop you always dreamed of? Would you spend your evenings volunteering at a local public radio station? What is your dream? What did you put on hold for "later?" It's never too late when God leads your journey. There is so much more to your history and your future than the period of your marriage. Because I know your Creator, I can confidently say there is a lot more left for you to achieve than what one relationship could ever reveal. Now that the relationship is over, what are you waiting for? Move on! Let it go! Only two things can happen from continuing to look behind you: Either you'll never get ahead, or you'll keep going off track!

When my father died I heard someone say, "One of the wealthiest places in the world is six feet underground." That sounded cruel to me, but it's true. So many hopes and ideas are buried, gone, never to be fulfilled. This is not to say that if you're married you can't fulfill your dreams, but taking hold of the time you have now, as you pursue a new life, is the perfect opportunity. Make it great. "Later" is now, so get your life in order and pursue your dreams. Take the steps necessary to achieve them. I wish you all the best on your journey.

> "Later" is now, so get your life in order and pursue your dreams.

Twelve

Steps to Recovery

~ What are you waiting for! ~

Need a little more encouragement? OK. You can start moving on from exactly where you are today. No matter what stage of recovery you're in, some form of mental shift is going to have to take place in order to carry you forward. Work from the inside out, not the outside in, because physical changes will always follow mental ones. Here is a group of key words and phrases I want you to become intimately familiar with:

The Mind	Let it Go
Refocus	Reinvent
Empower	Faith
Courage	Fresh Start

Write these words and phrases on index cards, "sticky" notes and message boards on your refrigerator. Place different words and phrases over your bed, in your wallet, near your computer at work, on the dashboard of your car and anywhere else where they will serve as reminders of the tools and resources you'll need to take on your new journey. Let me explain why...

~ The Mind...Change the Way You think ~

This truly is the starting point. Certain behavior always follows certain mental decisions: Recovery starts with the vision of recovery. This may sound like a cliché, but it's true. No climber reaches the top of a mountain, no millionaire earns a fortune, no builder constructs a home...without first conceiving the vision! Your mind is your most powerful weapon, and you have to use it to see yourself happy and content. One of my pastor's favorite sayings is, "Want a change, make a change." Sounds easy enough, right? Before you can make the change, however, you have to change your mind. That's where the plan of action takes place.

~ Let It Go ~

Drop it! Like a ball, a hot lump of coal or a sharp, prickly object in the hand. Quickly release it and dare not pick it up again. It's excess baggage that you need to stop carrying around. Release the one who hurt you, misused you, abandoned you or overlooked you. Cut the invisible chord that you've used to keep yourself tied to her or him. Don't carry that weight around any longer than necessary. Forget what lies behind and move forward to what lies ahead.

~ Refocus ~

If you could think of one single time that you'd categorize as the best day of your life (other than your wedding day), what would it be? Maybe the day you got on the scale after months of dieting and it registered 25 fewer pounds. Or maybe your graduation day, because when you were knee-deep in term papers and pulling all-nighters to study for exams, you never thought the day would come. It doesn't have to be an event. Maybe it's the day when you purchased that special gadget you'd been promising to buy for yourself. How did it make you feel? What did you think about life at that moment? No doubt, life felt good. You were happy. Landmark that day right now in your thought process and use it to refocus. Live as if your journey begins from that moment and remember it again every day, in place of the thoughts of regret, disappointment and anger that may be troubling you. Have that special moment again every day and you will open yourself to many others.

~ Reinvent yourself ~

Albert Einstein defined insanity as doing the same thing over and over again, and expecting different results. This is a new you! You're different now! Life experiences, good and bad, change us. Accept and embrace the things you've learned from this latest challenge. You've probably discovered something inside that you had no idea existed. Reinvent the possibilities of what you can do and become now that you've made the discovery.

~ Empower yourself ~

As if you've been fed a surge of energy, you have just received the authority to do whatever you desire. Don't wait for a pat on the back from someone else to start using this power. Empowerment builds confidence and self-esteem. You've learned you're responsible for your own choices. Why? Because the power is in the choices you make.

~ Faith ~

I've already shared how my faith in God helped get me through my divorce. Live by faith in God and in yourself everyday. Faith moves mountains and obstacles resistant to leaving your life.
"Faith is the assurance of things hoped for. "

~ Courage ~

None of this is easy. Most things of any value in life aren't easy. It takes courage to embrace the unfamiliar. Those who've succeeded in life have shown courage and taken risks. Sometimes the risks work out, sometimes not. It builds character and confidence. The reward is not always in the outcome, but in the growth that comes from taking a risk.

~ Make A Fresh Start ~

Now you're ready for it! It's time to do something new. You can do it! Go out and reintroduce yourself to a world were only the sky is the limit. Walk with your head held high, your chest out full of confidence in the new you.

About Us

Divorce Recovery Today, Inc.

We're tailor made for you. Divorce Recovery Today, Inc. is an organization committed to those who have been affected by a painful divorce or a difficult marriage. We are committed to helping individuals rebuild their lives and get on the road to recovery. We believe ALL your needs can and should be met. Divorce Recovery Today is for those who want to push past the pain and make a FRESH START! Services include workshops, group counseling and more.

To schedule Ms Williams for a book signing, workshop or conference speaker, contact her at drtrecovery@comcast.net.

For additional information, visit our website at:
DivorceRecoveryToday.com